9.0 Cascadia Earthquake Survival

How to Survive the Coming Megathrust Quake That Will Devastate the Pacific Northwest

by Damian Brindle

===> Get dozens of free survival guides, hundreds of videos, 600+ "how to" articles, gear reviews and so much more here: https://rethinksurvival.com

Disclaimer

The material covered within is for informational purposes only. I take no responsibility for what you do with this knowledge and I cannot be held responsible for any property or medical damages caused by the items or information you read about within. I would advise you to check your local laws as it's possible that some of the items or advice I offer may be illegal in some areas, and I would highly advise you against their use in said areas. Moreover, by using any information or material found within, you assume all risks for the material covered. You agree to indemnify, hold harmless, and defend the author, Damian Brindle, from all claims and damages arising from the use, possession or consequences of the information covered. By taking and/or using any informational resources found within, you agree that you will use this information in a safe and legal manner, consistent with all applicable laws, safety rules, and good common sense. You further agree that you will take such steps as may be reasonably necessary or required by applicable law to keep any information out of the hands of minors as well as untrained and/or irresponsible individuals.

Table of Contents

Introduction (Notes to Readers, Plus Free Stuff)

This book is intended to provide useful, actionable survival strategies as quickly as possible. As such, it's written to be fast to read and includes minimal product images. Links are provided to specific products should you want additional information or to purchase the product.

Please also realize that I use the terms "megaquake," "megathrust quake," and "Cascadia event" interchangeably, but they all reference the same disaster.

About Website Links

Realize, too, that this was originally written to be an electronic book only with many website links referenced throughout. Because this is a paperback book, however, referencing these links can be tedious if you had to type them into your web browser by hand. To make this easier on you, I have consolidated all referenced links into one page here: https://rethinksurvival.com/books/earthquake-links.html.

When new links are introduced they will be referenced with superscripts which will then correspond to the appropriate URL on the above referenced website page.

For completeness, however, all referenced links will also be included in Appendix B.

How This Book Is Organized

To help you get the information you want and need as quickly as possible, this book is split into three distinct parts:

Part 1: Earthquake Science. We'll start with understanding the science behind a Cascadia event, including why earthquakes form, how they're measured (and why it matters), why the Cascadia megaquake is different than any "normal" earthquake, and plenty more. Personally, I find this stuff fascinating, but you may not. If so, skip this section and come back to it later... the other two parts are more important to your survival anyway.

Part 2: The Cascadia Disaster. This is where you'll get to know what to expect when the Cascadia quake strikes, specifically all the destruction that will result from it. You'll be surprised at what can happen from this single event and, in my opinion, you really need to understand what's possible so that you'll then choose to act. But, again, if you're pressed for time or don't want to hear how bad things can get, move on to part three to find out what you can do to prepare yourself properly.

Part 3: Survival Solutions. Here's where we get into the solutions that I encourage you to take. Although I would strongly suggest that you start with part two first so that you'll know why these solutions make sense, the recommendations herein will help you to get prepared today because, after all, that's the entire purpose of this book.

Grab Your Free 30-Point Checklist

Odds are that you won't remember everything discussed when you're done reading this book. To make your life easier I've created a free, easy-to-reference 30-point safety checklist which you can download that outlines everything discussed herein. You'll find a link to it here (so that you can follow along if you like) as well as at the end of this book in Appendix A, but please do read the entire book first.

Now, download your free, easy-to-reference 30-point earthquake safety checklist here.[1]

Prepare Yourself for Natural Disaster in Only 5 Minutes

Since you clearly understand the need for earthquake safety, I want to share with you my unique **5 Minute Survival Blueprint** where you'll discover just how to keep your family safe and secure from disasters of all kinds in only 5 minutes a day, fast, easy, and inexpensively.[2]

More Survival Books You'll Enjoy

If you liked what you read when finished, you can find more survival books I've written at rethinksurvival.com/kindle-books.[3]

This Book's Tone

As noted before, this book is written in a quick, simple, easy to read format. Hence, it is presented in a "Conversational" form and not one that is intended to be grammatically correct. Getting YOU and your family ready for emergencies is the sole focus of this book.

And My Thanks...

I also want to thank those folks who took the time to review this book, to offer their own suggestions, and to correct my mistakes... you know who you are.

My Experiences Living in "Earthquake Country"

California is sometimes known as "earthquake country" and where I grew up (in the San Francisco Bay Area) earthquakes were commonplace. So much so, in fact, that I'm sure few people bothered to get out of bed for a magnitude 3.0 quake or smaller. Eventually, we moved away when I was in high school, but I still have family there and now live in the Pacific Northwest... a far more dangerous place to be, as you'll soon see.

Ever since I was a child, California residents have been warned that the San Andreas fault was going to unleash "The Big One" someday. This is the earthquake that will supposedly level cities up and down the coastline of California, possibly even causing the entire state to sink into the Pacific Ocean as some have claimed, which is impossible as this site explains why.[4]

Ludicrous claims aside, I should point out that the northern section of the San Andreas fault did erupt with force in 1906, devastating a fledgling San Francisco.[5] That earthquake was an estimated 7.9 on the Moment magnitude scale (MMS) with up to 3,000 people dead as a result and 80% of the city destroyed after fires raged on for several days. The southern section of the San Andreas fault, however, has yet to fully erupt recently which surely spells trouble for Los Angeles and San Diego residents alike when it does.

The 1989 Loma Prieta earthquake (also along San Andreas fault line) was my wakeup call.[6] Though I was a teenager at the time, I still vividly remember the devastation that this relatively weak magnitude 6.9

MMS earthquake (originally estimated to be 7.1 on the Richter scale) caused, particularly the double-decker Nimitz freeway collapse:

Figure 1

I recall watching the news, night after night, as rescue workers diligently toiled away to save those who were trapped within. And they did an amazing job saving lives. Unbelievably, only 63 people died because of this earthquake, the majority of which died during the initial collapse of the Nimitz freeway. Now, as you might suspect, this earthquake doesn't even come close to making the list of deadliest earthquakes in recorded history, but it does make the top 10 deadliest in U.S. history.[7,8]

As you'll soon see, earthquakes along the San Andreas are "small potatoes" when compared to a Cascadia event. Whereas the San Andreas is expected to unleash "The Big One" upon California someday, the Cascadia fault line is expected to unleash what the media has dubbed "The Really Big One" upon the Pacific Northwest... and possibly very soon.

You'd best be ready.

PART 1

Earthquake Science You Should Know

Before we get into what the Cascadia event is specifically, you should understand a bit about earthquakes first, including how they form, how they're measured, where they're most likely to occur and why. Let's tackle those questions one at a time...

How Earthquakes Form (And Why It Mostly Doesn't Matter)

The simplest explanation for most earthquakes I can give is this: the earth's crust is made up of several to a dozen major tectonic plates—as well as many smaller ones—all of which sit atop the earth's mantle and move around relative to each other at a rate of less than several inches per year; that may not sound like a lot of movement but, for large tectonic plates, it sure is. Often, the plates get stuck on one another, and when they get "unstuck" massive energy is released and earthquakes result.

Most of the time these earthquakes are harmless. In fact, this video points out that there are an estimated 500,000 earthquakes worldwide per year, 100,000 of which can be felt, with only 100 causing real damage.[9] An even smaller fraction of those 100 have the potential to cause massive damage.

Earthquake Classification Terms to Know

Scientists classify earthquakes as **tectonic** due to the tectonic plate movement discussed above (these are also the type of quake we're most concerned with here), **volcanic** because a volcano erupted and caused an earthquake, **collapse** due to underground caverns or mines collapsing, and **explosion** such as from the detonation of a nuclear bomb.

Faults are further classified as **normal** or **reverse** depending on whether the hanging wall moves up or down relative to the foot wall when the plates get "unstuck," or **transcurrent** (aka., "strike-slip faults") meaning they're sliding past one another horizontally rather than moving up or down. They might also be classified as shallow or deep to make things even more confusing.

Focusing solely on tectonic earthquakes there are, in fact, multiple ways that these occur, including:

1. **subduction zone quake** – occurs when one tectonic plate is trying to move under or over another plate at a convergent plate boundary (the Cascadia event is one);
2. **divergent boundary quake** – occurs where the plates pull away from each other;
3. **transform boundary quake** – occurs where plates try to slide past each other horizontally (the San Andreas fault is one of these).

This video gives a good example of how plates move relative to each other, how that causes earthquakes, and will quite possibly make you hungry for easy cheese and graham crackers because that's what he uses as the demonstration medium.[10]

There are also different types of seismic waves generated because of earthquakes, such as "S-waves" and "P-waves," among others, all of which help scientists figure out where the earthquake's epicenter is located using seismographs. Note: scientists are now more accurately pinpointing the "hypocenter," which is the epicenter, but in three-dimensional space.

Honestly, most of the above doesn't matter when it comes to earthquake survival because "shaking is shaking," and "damage is damage" no matter the cause. Regardless, you should at least be aware of the terminology when we discuss the Cascadia megathrust quake.

How Earthquakes Are Measured (And Why Small Changes in Magnitude Matter)

I won't go into excruciating detail about how earthquakes are measured. Suffice it to say that they're measured on a scale of one to ten, with ten being the worst possible scenario and one being... don't bother to get out of bed.

As eluded to previously, earthquakes are no longer measured on the Richter scale which you may have learned about as child but, rather, on the Moment magnitude scale because the Richter scale wasn't able to properly measure earthquakes at a far distance.[11, 12]

The important part to know about either measurement system is that a small increase in magnitude can drastically increase the energy released. That's because both systems are calculated on a logarithmic scale, rather than a linear one.

This is crucial to understand because being measured on a logarithmic scale means that a magnitude 2.0 quake is NOT merely twice as strong as a magnitude 1.0 quake but, rather, thirty-two times as strong. Worse, a magnitude 3.0 quake is 1000 times as strong as a magnitude 1.0 quake!

So, if we were to compare an assumed magnitude 9.0 Cascadia earthquake to the magnitude 6.8 Loma Prieta earthquake of 1989 discussed previously, we would not only find that the magnitude 9.0 is more than 158 times bigger, but almost 2000 times stronger (in terms of energy release). This USGS calculator makes these types of calculations a snap.[13]

You might be thinking, "Wait a minute, didn't we just say that a difference of 2.0 in magnitude was 1000 times stronger, but now you're saying that a difference of 2.2 in magnitude (9.0-6.8) is almost double that?" Yes, that's exactly what I'm saying, and this is precisely why the logarithmic measurement scale is so important to understand when it comes to anticipating earthquake energy release and the resulting damage. Small changes in magnitude make a big difference in both, especially with ever-larger differences in magnitude.

If you're curious, the largest earthquake in recorded history (measurements started around the year 1900) struck Chile in 1960 and measured between magnitude 9.4-9.6 which, if we assumed it was a magnitude 9.4, would be 398 times bigger than the Loma Prieta earthquake, yet 7943 times stronger, and if it were a magnitude 9.6, would be 630 times bigger and 15,848 times stronger.[14] Those numbers are very hard for me to wrap my imagination around.

Finally, as a reference, the earthquake that struck off the coast of Japan in 2011 was a magnitude 9.1 and the one that hit Indonesia in 2004 was estimated between magnitude 9.1-9.3, both of which caused massive damage and, worse, brought devastating tsunamis.

Why Earthquakes Occur So Frequently Along the Pacific Coastline

As you may already know, most earthquakes occur along large tectonic plate boundaries, as clearly indicated by this map of worldwide earthquakes in 2017:

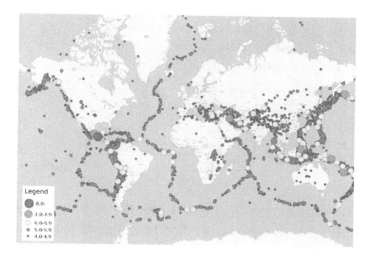

Figure 2

Now, if we look at the earthquake risk for only the United States we find this:

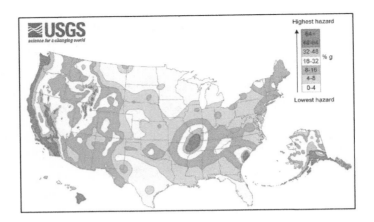

Figure 3

Not surprisingly, the highest hazard risk is along the entire Pacific coastline and parts of Alaska due to the Pacific plate and North American plate boundaries converging—as well as the Juan de Fuca plate—essentially running the entire length of the western United States coastline, Canada, Alaska, and part of Mexico.

If you live in the Midwest, specifically where Missouri, Illinois, Kentucky, Tennessee, and Arkansas meet, you may be wondering why you're also at significant risk. I did because I used to live there. As it turns out, the New Madrid Seismic Zone (NMSZ) is located there. What confuses scientists is that, "...there is no obvious mechanism driving the seismic activity," as this site explains because there are no tectonic plate boundaries involved.[15]

The article goes on to propose that, "Between 700 million and 540 million years ago, what is now the North American Plate was being pulled apart as it broke away from a supercontinent. The plate failed to split completely, but geologists think that the event left scars below the NMSZ: a buried rift zone, where the rocks are weak and fractured, over plutons— blobs of dense igneous rock—that themselves rose from an upwelling of unusually dense lower crust."

To put it succinctly, some scientists claim that the North American plate was supposed to split apart, it didn't, now the plate is weakened, and we occasionally get earthquakes in that weak spot, which happens to be directly beneath the Midwest states.

The Cascadia Earthquake Demystified

Before we discuss the Cascadia event specifically, I should briefly point out that it's not the only potential seismic threat to those of us in the Pacific Northwest; we are, in fact, also subject to magnitude 6.5-7.0 deep earthquakes, as well as up to magnitude 7.5 shallow crustal-fault earthquakes as well. Therefore, to assume that the Cascadia event is the only concerning seismic event out there would be wrong. It is, however, the most destructive event facing us.

Now, suggesting that the coming Cascadia megathrust quake (also known as the Cascadia event) is "just another earthquake" would be like saying that an eruption of the Yellowstone Supervolcano is akin to the Mount St. Helens eruption in 1980. Besides being classified as a "volcanic eruption," they have little in common. The same can be said for a Cascadia event as compared to any typical earthquake, regardless of magnitude.

Not only will **a Cascadia megathrust quake be among the largest of any we've ever experienced here in the United States**, the devastation will be unlike anything we've ever encountered due to:

1. Massive population explosion (several million people live in the Seattle and Portland metropolitan areas alone);
2. Widespread urbanization (the last quake struck when very few people lived here);
3. Subpar building codes (even buildings built a few decades ago weren't constructed to withstand a megaquake);
4. Overdependence on systems of support (specifically, electricity to heat and cook with, water from the city, grocery stores for food, etc.).

Let's quickly look at the top 10 earthquakes to directly hit the United States—data taken from Wikipedia—so that you can get an understanding of what has historically occurred, sorted by magnitude.[16] Please note that the following data is NOT in table format because it may not show properly on some devices:

#1. 1964 Alaska earthquake and tsunami

Date: 3/27/1964
Location: Alaska
Magnitude: 9.2
Fatalities: 143

#2. 1700 Cascadia earthquake

Date: 1/26/1700
Location: Pacific NWST

Magnitude: 8.7–9.2
Fatalities: Unknown

#3. 1965 Rat Islands earthquake and tsunami

Date: 2/4/1965
Location: Alaska
Magnitude: 8.7
Fatalities: 0

#4. 1946 Aleutian Islands earthquake and tsunami

Date: 4/1/1946
Location: Alaska
Magnitude: 8.6
Fatalities: 165

#5. 1957 Andreanof Islands earthquake and tsunami

Date: 3/9/1957
Location: Alaska
Magnitude: 8.6
Fatalities: 0

#6. 1857 Fort Tejon earthquake

Date: 1/9/1857
Location: California
Magnitude: 7.9
Fatalities: 2

#7. 1868 Hawaii earthquake and tsunami

Date: 4/2/1868
Location: Hawaii
Magnitude: 7.9
Fatalities: 77

#8. 1906 San Francisco earthquake

Date: 4/18/1906
Location: California
Magnitude: 7.9
Fatalities: 3,000+

#9. 2002 Denali earthquake

Date: 11/3/2002
Location: Alaska
Magnitude: 7.9
Fatalities: 0

#10. 2014 Aleutian Islands earthquake

Date: 6/23/2014
Location: Alaska
Magnitude: 7.9
Fatalities: 0

As you can see, Alaska shows up quite a bit and, in fact, takes the next three spots beyond the top 10 list shown above. Most of the island earthquakes (Aleutian, Rat Islands, Andreanof) are all off the coast of Alaska, and the Denali earthquake was centered within Denali National Park, Alaska.

The only earthquakes from the above list that didn't originate very near Alaska are the two in California and one in Hawaii. Take special note, in particular, of the single Cascadia earthquake on the list above which directly affected the Pacific Northwest in 1700.

I should also point out that tsunamis are often associated with the largest earthquakes, though, for some reason the Wikipedia list didn't specifically state that a tsunami was also associated with the 1700 Cascadia earthquake too, because there was one.

Why Are All Quakes Near Alaska NOT Cascadia Events?

You might now be wondering why many of the earthquakes near Alaska are not classified as Cascadia events because, after all, they're located very near tectonic plate boundaries and in the same general area.

Well, as it turns out, a Cascadia event is a very specific earthquake that involves the Juan de Fuca plate (and to a lesser extent the even smaller Gorda and Explorer plates) and is highlighted purple in the image below:

Figure 4

Relative to the surrounding Pacific plate to the west and North American plate to the east, the Juan de Fuca plate is very small, and it's currently getting pushed underneath the North American plate by the Pacific plate, thereby creating a subduction zone:

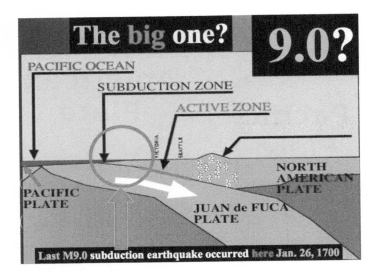

Figure 5

As you can see from the image above, a Cascadia event is known as a subduction zone earthquake because the Juan de Fuca plate is trying to slide under the North American plate.

The other big earthquakes near Alaska are not considered Cascadia events because they don't involve this specific interaction but, rather, the Pacific plate interacting with the North American plate— known as the Alaskan-Aleutian megathrust zone—or other plate interactions besides the Juan de Fuca and North American plates specifically.

Fortunately, many of the Alaskan-Aleutian megaquakes are relatively harmless because, as you might suspect, location is everything when it comes to the fallout from natural disasters... and earthquakes are no exception. The Cascadia event, on the other hand, is in precisely the wrong spot to cause maximum damage here in the Pacific Northwest, as we'll soon uncover.

How Often Do Cascadia Events Occur?

Clearly, the next logical question to answer is how often these Cascadia earthquakes occur because, if they only occur once ever million years and the last one was in 1700, then you and I have almost nothing to worry about. Sadly, that's not the case.

The short answer is that they occur every 250-500 years on average. This site points out that the range of occurrence can vary widely: "The most recent magnitude 9 Cascadia megaquake struck in the year 1700 — a date verified by tree-ring dating and historic accounts of the tsunami, which crossed the Pacific and hit Japan. The evidence on land suggests the entire Northwest coast gets slammed every 500 years, on average — though the intervals between quakes have ranged from a few hundred to nearly a thousand years. But evidence from seafloor cores suggests that the southern half of the fault — off the Oregon and Northern California coast — is much more dangerous, rupturing every 250 years."[17]

The same article goes on to state that, "In recent years, Oregon State University researcher Chris

Goldfinger has collected dozens of additional cores, which he says show evidence of 19 quakes of magnitude 9 or greater that ripped the entire length of the subduction zone in the past 10,000 years." Do some math and the data suggests a megathrust quake of magnitude 9.0 or greater occurs every 500 years.

So, you might be saying to yourself, "What's the worry? We've got nearly 200 years to go!" Not quite, since averages can be very misleading when it comes to predicting natural disasters. It's really the range that we should be concerned with, and scientists suggest the range can be anywhere from about 200 years to 1000 years, and we're most certainly within that range.

Now, if we add in very large earthquakes as well (those with magnitude 8.3-8.6 but not quite a 9.0) then that nearly doubles the number of devastating earthquakes in the past 10,000 years and, therefore, halves the original average to about one megaquake every 250 years.

Moreover, this site states that, "The calculated odds that a Cascadia earthquake will occur in the next 50 years range from 7 percent to 15 percent for a great earthquake affecting the entire Pacific Northwest to about 37 percent for a very large earthquake affecting Southern Oregon and Northern California."[18] Personally, I'm neither a betting man nor do I put a lot of faith in estimates like these. Regardless, those estimates are high enough that we should prepare for the possibility of a Cascadia event in our lifetimes.

What is a Megathrust Quake?

You've heard me mention a "megathrust" quake a few times now, so let's explain what that means. This Wikipedia article puts it best: "Megathrust earthquakes occur at subduction zones at destructive convergent plate boundaries, where one tectonic plate is forced underneath another. These interplate earthquakes are the planet's most powerful, with moment magnitudes (Mw) that can exceed 9.0. Since 1900, all earthquakes of magnitude 9.0 or greater have been megathrust earthquakes. No other type of known terrestrial source of tectonic activity has produced earthquakes of this scale."[19]

If you'll recall, the Juan de Fuca plate is attempting to subduct under the North American plate which is a convergent plate boundary. As a result, we get a highly active megathrust quake location. And, as I've said before, location is everything when it comes to the destruction caused by a megathrust quake. Whereas many megaquakes are relatively harmless (such as the Alaskan-Aleutian megathrust zone), others will cause widespread devastation, and the Cascadia megathrust zone is one of those devastating locations.

How Big is the Cascadia Fault?

The Cascadia subduction zone (or Cascadia fault) is a 620-mile-long fault approximately 50 miles offshore at its nearest point that stretches from the Northern Vancouver Islands to Northern California, covering all of Oregon and Washington states:

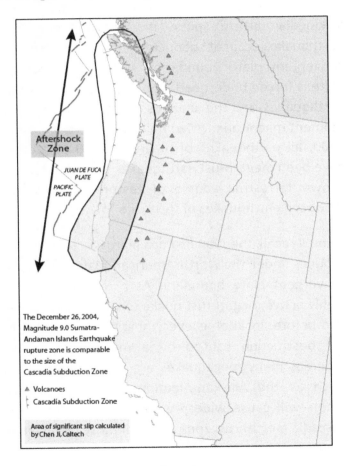

Figure 6

For what it's worth, the fault is divided into northern and southern sections, with the northern section having slipped during the year 1700 quake. This may suggest that the southern section is the next to slip, but who really knows for sure. I can say that the USGS scientists seems to think so, because the "area of significant" slip shown in the image above points to the southern section of the fault.

That said, this article points out that scientists have: "...observed very compact sediments offshore of Washington and northern Oregon [which is part of the northern section of the fault line] that could support earthquake rupture over a long distance and close to the trench, which increases both earthquake and tsunami hazards."[20]

The article continues: "Offshore of Washington and northern Oregon, ocean floor sediments are much more compact than in central Oregon—indicating that sediments are less porous and have less water between the grains. That all adds up to a disaster about to happen, according to the study, which was led by the University of Texas at Austin and published in Nature Geoscience." Northern Oregon and Washington residents should not let their guard down.

Let me throw one more worrisome event at you, just to keep you on your toes...

Puget Sound Slow Slip: The Catalyst That Could Set Cascadia Off

Unbeknownst to many, the Puget Sound experiences a "slow slip" event on a routine basis. According to this site, "The event happens about every 14 months deep underneath the Puget Sound area and is essentially a slow earthquake that takes place over the course of two weeks."[21]

The article continues: "Seismologists often refer to this as a 'straw that broke the camel's back' scenario. 'It's loading up the edge of the lock zone of the Cascadia subduction zone more rapidly than normal tectonic processes would do,' explained Bill Steele, director of communications at the [Pacific Northwest Seismic Network] PNSN. 'You're getting seven months of strain accumulation applied to the back edge of the fault over a week.'"

Luckily, the probability of a Cascadia event only slightly increases during this two-week "slow slip" timeframe. That said, if you're ultra-paranoid then you can watch the hourly tremor map which tracks this very scenario, though, I wouldn't obsess over it.[22]

Supercomputer Damage Simulations Vary Widely

By now you must be wondering, "How much damage can we really expect from a Cascadia event?" I'll share my own thoughts shortly but, for now, scientists attempted to answer that very question not too long ago. In 2017, the University of Washington ran fifty simulations of how a Cascadia event might unfold as part of a larger M9 Project, "... [which is] a team of experts whose goal is to reduce catastrophic potential effects of a Cascadia megathrust earthquake on social, built, and natural environments through the advancement of methodologies, early warnings, and community planning."[23]

"The team presented both best- and worst-case scenarios of a potential 9.0 earthquake on the Cascadia subduction zone at the Geological Society of America's annual meeting on October 24. Their 50 simulations use different factor combinations, such as where the epicenter may be, how far inland the earthquake would travel, and where along the fault the shaking would be the strongest... this is the most in-depth scenario prediction to date, The Independent reported," according to this article.[24]

"'Surprisingly, Seattle experiences less severe shaking if the epicenter is located just beneath the tip of northwest Washington... The reason is because the rupture is propagating away from Seattle, so it's most affecting sites offshore. But when the epicenter is located pretty far offshore, the rupture travels inland and all of that strong ground shaking piles up on its way to Seattle, to make the shaking in Seattle much stronger,'" from this interview with Dr. Erin Wirth.[25]

She goes on to state: "Overall, the results confirm that coastal areas would be hardest hit, and locations in sediment-filled basins like downtown Seattle would shake more than hard, rocky mountaintops. But within that general framework, the picture can vary a lot; depending on the scenario, the intensity of shaking can vary by a factor of 10. But none of the pictures is rosy."

A Note on the Seasonal Timing of a Cascadia Event

There is something to be said for the timing of such an event, at least, with regards to the damage from the initial megaquake. John Bauer from Oregon's Department of Geology and Mineral Industries was quoted as saying: "'The best case would be say, summertime... Folks are outside enjoying themselves. They're not in buildings. Worst case is we're in schools and our workplaces and it has been quite wet.' In the rainy season there would be more landslides and building collapses. If the quake happens at night, more people survive because they're sleeping in wooden homes that flex during the shaking."[26]

Personally, I'm not so sure how much safer we'll be inside our homes as opposed to anywhere else. There may be something to people being safer inside a wooden home as opposed to a rigid building but, then again, a lot will depend on how well-built any structure is with regards to survivability inside them, as we'll soon see.

And what about where people will be spending their time during the summer months, if that's supposedly the best timing? Here in the Pacific Northwest, I'd suspect many folks will be near the water, particularly the coastline and beaches, which is precisely where you don't want to be not long after the initial quake due to the high likelihood of destructive tsunami waves following shortly thereafter. And, of course, there will be more tourists around—especially along the beaches—so, I'm not convinced that summer will be the best scenario for timing. Unbelievably, we may want it to rain... a lot; I'll explain why soon enough.

Can We Predict "The Really Big One" And What Warning Time Do We Have?

Although scientists ran simulations to better understand what we can expect after we're hit, this doesn't mean that we can predict such an earthquake, which means we'll have no warning time whatsoever, at least, as things stand currently.

The good news is that technology can help. This ShakeAlert system is one possibility: "Today, the technology exists to detect earthquakes, so quickly, that an alert can reach some areas before strong shaking arrives. The purpose of the ShakeAlert™

system is to identify and characterize an earthquake a few seconds after it begins, calculate the likely intensity of ground shaking that will result, and deliver warnings to people and infrastructure in harm's way."[27]

The website continues: "Studies of earthquake early warning methods in California have shown that the warning time would range from a few seconds to a few tens of seconds. ShakeAlert™ can give enough time to slow trains and taxiing planes, to prevent cars from entering bridges and tunnels, to move away from dangerous machines or chemicals in work environments and to take cover under a desk, or to automatically shut down and isolate industrial systems. Taking such actions before shaking starts can reduce damage and casualties during an earthquake. It can also prevent cascading failures in the aftermath of an event. For example, isolating utilities before shaking starts can reduce the number of fire initiations."

This article suggests that we could even get two or three minutes (others suggest up to five minutes) of warning for a Cascadia event with such alert systems.[28] I know that doesn't sound like much, but even a minute or two is enough for a wide variety of mitigating actions to happen as noted previously, and it is certainly enough time for you to find the safest place to take cover wherever you are.

The bad news is that the system is not yet available to the American public, though it's apparently widely used in Japan where people can get warnings on their cell phones.[29] Eventually, the system will be in widespread use and available to the public in the Pacific Northwest but don't expect that to be anytime soon and, even then, the warning system can't stop most of the damage. You still need to be ready for the aftermath.

Early warning systems aside, I found an interesting article that indicated the sound emitted by rocks, of all things, could provide up to a week's notice: "A recent paper in the Geophysical Research Letters journal outlines what could be the most advanced method yet for detecting earthquakes well ahead of time—giving people days, rather than moments, to find safety. The paper describes a computer program that eavesdrops on quiet rumbles made by rocks deep inside the Earth. Scientists have long known about these sounds but until now haven't found a deeper pattern in them. 'What happens before an earthquake is that rocks emit noise because one grain of rock is rubbing against another grain of rock,' co-author Colin Humphreys, a materials scientist at Cambridge University, told Reuters. 'It's a little like a squeaky door.'"[30]

Now, that would be something if scientists can make use of that type of information in the future and do so without sounding false alarms in the process.

Reiterating The 12 Major Facts That We've Discovered

Let's take a moment to briefly recap what we've discovered thus far before we discuss the coming devastation of the Cascadia megathrust quake:

1. Earthquakes occur along the Pacific coast because of plate tectonics; this is usually the interaction of the Pacific plate and North American plate, but also the much smaller Juan de Fuca plate, which is the central concern for us.

2. Earthquakes are measured using the Magnitude momentum scale where even small differences in magnitude can make a big difference in the energy released and, therefore, the destruction involved.

3. The Cascadia event is a subduction zone quake, meaning that the Juan de Fuca plate is being pushed underneath the North America plate.

4. Location is critical to the devastation expected; many megathrust earthquakes cause no damage at all due to their location, but the Cascadia zone is placed perfectly to

cause maximum damage to the Pacific Northwest.

5. A Cascadia event occurs on average every 250-500 years, but ranges from about 200 years to 1000 years with the last one occurring in 1700, more than 300 years ago.

6. The most recent Cascadia earthquake was estimated to be magnitude 8.7-9.2, with most historical seafloor records indicating they're magnitude 9.0 or greater.

7. The Cascadia fault line runs more than 600 miles along the Pacific Northwest coastline and is split into northern and southern sections, with the southern section anticipated by the USGS to be the next to go, which directly affects all residents of Oregon, southern Washington, and northern California.

8. Recent studies indicate that compact sediment further north along the fault could indicate rupture over a longer distance, thereby directly affecting most of the Pacific Northwest residents, including all of Washington and British Columbia.

9. The Puget Sound Slow Slip (which occurs every 14 months) could be the catalyst that sets off the Cascadia megathrust quake, but probably not. Stop stressing about it.

10. Simulations are great and help us to understand what may occur, but you still need

to prepare for the aftermath regardless. Major metropolitan areas will be hit hard, coastal areas will be hit harder.

11. Timing of the event may have a strong impact on death tolls—summertime is anticipated to be the best time, spring is the worst—though, I'm not convinced that's going to be true.

12. Coming warning systems will help mitigate last-minute damage and save lives, but they won't stop most of the destruction and are not yet in widespread use.

PART 2

Why the Cascadia Megathrust Quake Will Devastate the Pacific Northwest

I'm sure that if you've ever lived where earthquakes occur often, or even if you've just seen the devastation afterwards, you may be thinking that a Cascadia event is just going to a bigger version of whatever you've seen before.

On the one hand, that's true. The Cascadia event will be bigger, but it will also bring new perils not typically associated with "normal" earthquakes. Before I discuss those, however, let's first understand how much worse the shaking alone from a Cascadia megathrust quake will be...

How Much Worse the Shaking Will Be (As Well as the Destruction from It)

Kenneth Murphy, who directs FEMA's Pacific Northwest response was once quoted as saying: "**Our operating assumption is that everything west of Interstate 5 will be toast**," during this 2015 The New Yorker interview.[31] What a statement! It sure made me sit up and take notice.

The same article goes on to state that: "Ian Madin, who directs the Oregon Department of Geology and

Mineral Industries (DOGAMI), estimates that seventy-five per cent of all structures in the state [of Oregon] are not designed to withstand a major Cascadia quake. FEMA calculates that, across the region, something on the order of a million buildings—more than three thousand of them schools—will collapse or be compromised in the earthquake. So will half of all highway bridges, fifteen of the seventeen bridges spanning Portland's two rivers, and two-thirds of railways and airports; also, one-third of all fire stations, half of all police stations, and two-thirds of all hospitals."

Read that quote again if you breezed through it because those words should open your eyes to what's coming. Granted, estimates are estimates, not facts. Who knows for sure just how big the next Cascadia event will be or precisely what devastation will result.

Unfortunately, many building, schools, and bridges in the Pacific Northwest simply weren't designed or built with the expectation to withstand the shaking from a very large earthquake. The New Yorker article referenced above was one that really woke me up to the fact that a Cascadia megaquake will bring widespread devastation, much more so than any earthquake I've ever experienced.

We can say, however, that there will be a much greater chance of widespread destruction due to the length of time that buildings will be subject to earthquake stresses from a megathrust earthquake. Why? Because these don't last merely for seconds as most earthquakes do, they last for minutes... and that makes a big difference in the destructive aftermath.

To give you a few examples of how long earthquakes can last, the 2001 magnitude 9.1 earthquake that hit Japan lasted six minutes. The 2004 magnitude 9.1 (some estimate it was up to a 9.3) earthquake that hit Indonesia and surrounding areas lasted eight to ten minutes. One megathrust quake was estimated to last up to fifteen minutes!

Can you imagine that? I swore fifteen seconds felt like a long time during the Loma Prieta earthquake, fifteen minutes may feel like the world is ending. Even a few minutes would feel like an eternity.

Feelings aside, it's the continual stresses placed upon a building—especially "stick-built" homes—that are the real problem. If you're unaware, many homes in the United States are built, by and large, with inexpensive lumber (e.g., 2x4's), plywood sheeting, some larger support beams, and nails. The outside walls are anchored to a concrete slab and everything else is attached to them in one way or another. Some walls are "load bearing," others are not. Roof designs vary, but most use rafters to hold the load in place; the roof is also attached to the outside walls which strengthens the entire design. Of course, there are plenty of exceptions to this generalization, but that's the basics of a typical "stick-built" suburban home.

No matter the design, so long as nothing moves around drastically most home designs are sturdy. But, when the home's foundation begins to shake, and walls move around laterally, those stresses are transferred throughout the building, thereby weakening attachment points. Over time, those attachment points get weaker and weaker, eventually failing. When the right (or should I say, wrong) attachment points fail then something, such as a wall or roof support, in this case, comes crashing down and everything gets worse from then on.

Let me illustrate this idea with a simple example. Imagine that you've driven a nail partway into a board, but you decided it was in the wrong spot. Rather than using a hammer to pry the nail out, you choose to use your fingers to wiggle it out. When you first grab the nail, it remains firmly in place. After a few seconds you may notice the nail moving a slight bit, and after several seconds the nail may begin to move even more. Eventually, the nail will move enough to come free. This is essentially what happens to your home during an earthquake. Over time the nails (as well as other anchor points) move enough that they come free and then the structure fails. It just takes time, and megathrust quakes provide the necessary time.

Soil Liquefaction Makes Damage Estimates Much Worse for Seattle and Portland

A formerly referenced article suggests that the average duration of shaking in Seattle is about 100 seconds.[32] Realize that's the average duration of shaking from their fifty simulations, it could be longer or shorter. Remember, too, that we've previously discovered the longest earthquakes lasted several minutes or longer, and that experts anticipate we could get "two or three minutes" of shaking which is significantly longer than the average of 100 seconds.

Now, considering that almost all typical earthquakes last less than thirty seconds at most and combined with the fact that about fifteen percent of Seattle is built on a questionable footing already due to a phenomenon known as soil liquefaction—which effectively turns hard ground into liquid—I would expect significant damage to the city, bridges, and roadways for sure.[33] (Note: if you live in Seattle, take the time to read this article to help you understand if where you live is constructed with unreinforced masonry, if it has been retrofitted, and more.[34])

During this interview, Scott Ashford of Oregon State College states that: "'For these large magnitude-9 earthquakes, we can see liquefaction over hundreds of square miles,' he says. 'And for us, that would mean as far as the I-5 corridor.'"[35] With that in mind, I don't want to ignore Portland just because I don't live there... you're subject to the same soil liquefaction problems as Seattle.

Soil liquefaction isn't only concerning because it means buildings are more likely to collapse. The concerns are much more than that. For example, during this interview, Tom Bearden says, "While surface structures settle, underground utilities tend to rise out of the ground."[36] Scott Ashford adds that: "When the ground turns into almost a viscous fluid, and when that takes place, a lot of our utilities like manholes, like sewer lines, will tend to float up out of the ground, and when something floats like that that's in the ground, it tends to break."

Did you catch all that? They're not merely saying that buildings will sink, but that underground utilities will rise and, subsequently, break. Wouldn't that be a sight to see? It sure would, and not a good sight to see either.

Clearly, there are many variables involved as to how bad things will be. Just don't expect the best-case scenario. Choose, instead, to plan for the worst-case scenario and hope for the best.

Building Design Matters a Lot

You might think that buildings aren't designed to move much, if at all. They're expected to stand up straight and to resist gravity. And that when the ground starts moving underneath, bad things happen to structures that aren't meant to move. If they're designed poorly, that's very true.

For example, here's a video of the magnitude 7.8 earthquake that hit Nepal in 2015 which killed almost 9000 people.[37] I've skipped ahead about a minute into the video, but if you watch for less than a minute from that point on you'll see what happens to buildings that weren't designed to move with earthquakes. Hint: they come crumbling down.

There are plenty of exceptions, of course, specifically building designs that allow large structures to sway laterally and even interesting building designs that use a curtain of cables to "tie down" the building, among other Japanese innovations.[38, 39] Clearly, Japan takes their building designs very seriously, as they should.

That said, I don't want you to think that we here, in American, don't take our building designs seriously, or that as soon as a large earthquake hits the Pacific Northwest that buildings come tumbling down three seconds later. That's not true either. We have some strict building codes as well, possibly even more strict than Japan does as this comparison points out.[40]

The good news is that, with the right building design, earthquakes—even big ones—probably won't take down well-designed large buildings. For example, here's some video footage of a tall building in Japan that started swaying during the 9.1 earthquake that hit Japan in 2011.[41] If you just watch the first thirty seconds, you'll see that the building swayed back and forth and stayed standing, which is great news, and precisely what the building was designed to do.

Of course, just because a building remained upright doesn't mean that major damage didn't occur both inside and out, it just means that you have a much better chance of survival because the building didn't fully collapse down on you.

And, remember, it's not just buildings that crumble, roadways do too when they're stressed beyond their design limits, so be aware of where you are if you're driving when it hits:

Figure 7

The Tsunami Waves That May Wash Away Whatever Survived

As if the damage from minutes of shaking aren't enough, a Cascadia event brings with it another huge force: devastating tsunami waves. Besides the massive amount of seawater brought inland where it doesn't belong, a tsunami tends to bring some debris with it too:

Figure 8

In some ways, the tsunami threat worries me more than the earthquake does because, assuming you were to survive crumbling buildings, you may then have to hightail it to higher ground if you live anywhere near the coastline.

In my case, my family and I live near the Puget Sound, almost on the water. It's a beautiful spot and we have no interest in moving. The potential problem we have where we currently live is that we're too close to sea level for comfort, at about 45 feet above zero-elevation. It wouldn't be much of a hike to significantly higher ground but, regrettably, there are other obstacles in our way, which I'll point out momentarily.

For those living near the coast, "Geologists have also determined the Pacific Northwest is not prepared for such a colossal quake. The tsunami produced could reach heights of 80 to 100 feet," according to this article, but could be as small as twenty feet in some areas.[42] Personally, I wouldn't want to be anywhere near a tsunami wave regardless of height.

Further inland, the waves may not loom large like they do in the movies, but they will bring serious flooding, deadly debris as shown above, as well as utter chaos to the entire landscape as this video and this one too from the 2011 Japanese tsunami plainly show.[43, 44]

As a comparison, the tsunami waves that hit Japan in 2011 (which is about the closest current example we have to compare to) "...reached run-up heights (how far the wave surges inland above sea level) of up to 128 feet (39 meters) at Miyako city and traveled inland as far as 6 miles (10 km) in Sendai. The tsunami flooded an estimated area of approximately 217 square miles (561 square kilometers) in Japan," according to this site.[45]

The Cascadia Tsunami Flooding May Not Be as Bad as in Japan

Scientists estimate that, "Seismic sea waves, or tsunamis, could be as high as thirty to forty feet with a magnitude 9 earthquake, but less than half that with an 8. Fifteen to thirty minutes after the mainshock had died away, the first of several tsunamis would strike. In some cases, the water would first rush out to sea, exposing sea floor never before seen as dry land, but a short time later, a wall of water would rush inland, sweeping the sand from barrier bars inland, overwhelming beach houses and bayfront boutiques and restaurants as far as several blocks away from the sea. These destructive waves would be repeated several times," according to this article.[46]

Their estimations indicate that the floods resulting from a Cascadia event may not be as bad as those seen in Japan in 2011. Regardless, flooding will cause widespread damage to infrastructure, severely delay response times to those most affected because of flooded out roadways, bring a huge mess of debris and contaminated floodwaters, and surely increase the spread of diseases as well due to lack of clean water, poor sanitation practices, overcrowding in shelters, and limited access to healthcare. Sadly, we could see outbreaks of typhoid fever, cholera, and dysentery, to name a few diseases nobody wants to contract.

I do want to mention that it's not just those along the coastline who could be affected. Anyone caught in narrow pathways, such as drainage entries, river channels, and especially flood plains may be directly impacted by tsunami flooding as well, since water will always take the path of least resistance until it runs out of momentum. This could be miles inland by some estimates.

And don't think that you can outrun these waves either. According to the Pacific Tsunami Warning Center (a great site to learn all about tsunamis, by the way): "Tsunami wave speed is controlled by water depth. Where the ocean is over 6,000 meters (3.7 miles) deep, unnoticed tsunami waves can travel at the speed of a commercial jet plane, over 800 km per hour (500 miles per hour). Tsunamis travel much slower in shallower coastal waters where their wave heights begin to increase dramatically."[47]

Close to land the waves will be much slower than that (roughly 10-20 mph), but only Usain Bolt may be able to outrun them. The question, therefore, is would he outlast them and, more importantly, could you? Probably not. Take a moment to read this article to understand why people are more likely to drown during a tsunami and hurricane than for any other reason.[48]

Finally, I do want to try and put your mind at ease if you live further away from the coast, especially near Seattle. Expert Sandi Doughton (a Seattle Times science writer) states that, "'The tsunami won't really be a factor in Seattle or Puget Sound... By the time the swell gets here, it will be pretty small,'" according to this article.[49] That would be good news for sure as it means many residents, such as myself, may not need to run for higher ground immediately after, though, there's likely no harm in doing so, just in case they're wrong.

Why the Devastation Gets Worse, Much Worse

Thus far we've seen that a clear majority of buildings and bridges—especially west of Interstate 5—will be heavily damaged, if not outright demolished from the initial megaquake. We've also discovered that coastal flooding from the resulting tsunami will devastate coastal cities and may even affect many of those living along major waterways (such as the Puget Sound) as well. Let's find out why this gets much worse than that right now...

Aftershocks

I've yet to mention that, as this site points out, we will see aftershocks which, "...are dangerous because they are usually unpredictable, can be of a large magnitude, and can collapse buildings that are damaged from the main shock. Bigger earthquakes have more and larger aftershocks and the sequences can last for years or even longer especially when a large event occurs in a seismically quiet area."[50]

Personally, I had no idea that aftershocks from a single event could last for years. The important takeaway is that we could have hundreds of them and that they "can be of a large magnitude, and can collapse buildings that are damaged from the main shock." So, assuming you and your home survived intact, you cannot therefore assume that you and your home are now safe merely because you survived the initial earthquake. For instance, your home could be structurally damaged in ways that you cannot see and, though it appeared to survive the initial quake, is now vulnerable to aftershocks, which means you shouldn't be in or even near it.

Moreover, aftershocks can cause additional landslides besides those that may have been triggered by the initial earthquake. Therefore, if you live anywhere near mountainous terrain (especially if you already know you live near a landslide hazard) be very aware of this potential additional concern.

Interestingly, large earthquakes in the weeks and months (even several months) preceding a Cascadia megathrust quake could indicate that "The Really Big One" is coming, though, probably not with enough certainty that you can take immediate action.

Regardless, this seismic activity is known as a "foreshock" earthquake. "A foreshock is an earthquake that occurs before a larger seismic event (the mainshock) and is related to it in both time and space. The designation of an earthquake as foreshock, mainshock or aftershock is only possible after the full sequence of events has happened," as this article points out.[51]

In other words, we could be hit with a large earthquake that was initially assumed to be "the event," only to find out that an aftershock was even bigger and later classified as the mainshock event! Unfortunately, this site suggests that, "In the Pacific Northwest, there is no evidence of foreshock activity for most historic earthquakes," which makes any hope of a relatively smaller warning quake unlikely.[52]

Anyway, like I said from the start, the devastation continues to get worse, and here's why...

Falling Trees

For those of us who live in the Pacific Northwest, specifically west of the Cascades, we know that the landscape is littered with pine trees. Where I live I'm surrounded by them and many people I know are too. The problem is that when a megaquake hits, some of these pine trees will topple as a result. They just can't help it because of their shallow root system.

Granted, there are other factors involved as to whether a tree will topple, but I've seen more than one tree fall over merely because of high winds passing through the area. Just imagine how unstable these trees will be when the ground shakes ferociously for minutes on end! Even if they don't completely topple over from the roots up, many large tree branches could break away and tops of trees may snap off, none of which is good for your health or your home's structural integrity.

That said, I could be "crying wolf" here. There is evidence that trees are sturdier than I fear. For example, this video shows a line of oak trees along the San Andreas fault doing just fine during a 2004 magnitude 6.0 earthquake.[53] Regardless, a magnitude 6.0 is nothing like a magnitude 9.0... and several seconds of shaking is nothing like several minutes. You'll have to decide how bad this could get where you live.

Power Lines

One thing I know for sure is this: if where you live has above-ground power lines, be concerned. Even if the trees don't topple right over, they'll surely knock down power lines left and right because of swaying trees and falling tree branches. Many power lines may just come down on their own without any assistance from toppled trees.

This will surely cause massive power outages but, perhaps more importantly, they may cause widespread fires. At the very least, downed power lines will be a danger to drive or walk over—here's why you should never cross downed power lines—and, in many cases, may make it impossible for you to evacuate as you expected to.[54] Look at this intersection of power lines and other cables near my own neighborhood:

Figure 9

As you can see, there are quite a few cables strung up at this intersection, and I didn't even do a great job of capturing the entire area in that photo. There are power lines behind me in the photo, down each street to the left and right, and everywhere you look, to be frank.

If that mess of cables came down, you would have three choices:

1. Drive or walk over it and hope nothing is energized (that's not the best plan at all);
2. Find an alternate route and hope you can get out (there's one other way to drive out, but there are plenty of power lines in that direction as well);
3. Completely abandon the roadways, choosing to traverse woodlands by foot (this is perhaps the only, mostly plausible option left).

Perhaps there's a fourth option: stay put. In my case, though, moving to higher ground is probably the best choice and likely is for you as well. You'll have to decide for yourself what the best course of action is where you live and for your situation.

Without a doubt, not everyone is going to have the same problem that I and my neighbors do. Some people live in homes that aren't surrounded by trees, though many do. Others may have below-ground power lines, which is great news. The point is that if an earthquake did strike, downed power lines will be a major problem for many people, me included. And, even if you don't have above-ground power lines next to your home, odds are that they will be along major roadways in your town, so don't expect to get very far by vehicle in any case.

Natural Gas Pipelines

Many people prefer natural gas for a variety of reasons, including cost, reliability, and environmental-friendliness. Those benefits aside, you should expect numerous fires from gas leaks after an earthquake. In fact, this site states that, "Natural gas piping and appliances can be damaged during earthquakes, causing gas leaks. If ignited, this can result in fires which can burn part of, or, the entire building. About one in four fires after an earthquake is related to natural gas leaks. Gas leaks after an earthquake are more likely if: (1) There are structural weaknesses, (2) Gas appliances are not anchored, (3) Flexible pipe connections are not used."[55]

There are a few actions you can take beforehand to mitigate the potential for fire resulting from a natural gas leak after an earthquake, including flexible appliance connectors, automatic gas shutoff valves, and simply knowing how to turn off the main gas line to your home. You'll want to have the proper tool to do so safely.[56]

Unfortunately, the odds are that plenty of homeowners and business owners near you won't have done the same and you'll still be subject to widespread fires as a result. This scenario is even more likely with a megathrust earthquake due to the greater damage to infrastructure expected, especially when utility pipes and cables are literally being thrust out of the ground as stated previously.

Remember, too, that "where there's fire, there is smoke" to turn a well-known proverb around. Expect air quality problems, including difficulty breathing and even poor visibility if fires rage on long enough. Moreover, we should assume that first responders will be overwhelmed with calls, that some—if not a majority—of their equipment will be damaged, and that critical infrastructure (such as water main lines) will be damaged as well. All of this adds up to make a timely response to fires nearly impossible, if they'll even be able to respond at all.

Widespread Infrastructure and Contamination Concerns

As you might suspect, if we're expecting problems with power lines and natural gas lines, odds are pretty good that we're going to have problems with other infrastructure or "systems of support" as I like to call them, especially water lines, sewer lines, roads, bridges, oil refineries, the Olympic Pipeline (which runs through Seattle and Portland) as well as a variety of food and medicine distribution centers... you name it. Basically, everything you and I rely upon will be affected somehow and, in some cases, possibly even destroy the environment for decades (e.g., oil refineries and pipelines), let alone being all but useless to authorities and residents alike.

In fact, FEMA anticipates both "hazardous material releases and contaminated water supplies," as briefly noted here.[57] It bears repeating that drinking water supplies (as well as any water source you might encounter in the aftermath) could quickly become infested with several nasty diseases for a variety of reasons, including contamination from floodwaters and the debris they bring, broken water and sewer mainlines, damaged or down water or sewer treatment plants, and even massive hazardous material spills all throughout the region.

Though several years old now, this Washington Military Hazardous Materials Profile PDF file is a real eye-opener too.[58] In that guide they discuss many types of hazards, such as oil spills, meth labs (who knew they were that big of a problem here), and radioactive material spills, to name a few, all of which pose a hazard to the population on an everyday basis whether we're aware of them or not.

Sadly, the Hanford Nuclear site in southern Washington state is known as "the most toxic place in America," according to this article.[59] What happens to nearby residents if that site is severely affected by a megaquake? Nothing good, that's for sure. Fortunately, Hanford is quite a way east of the coastline, so maybe it won't be affected, but who really knows until the megaquake and aftershocks strike.

I haven't even mentioned Oregon yet. While Washington state does have some oil refineries (that's not necessarily a good thing if the earthquake destroys them) Oregon doesn't have any oil refineries. Instead, they get their oil from outside the state. The problem with this is that: "There are no fuel refineries in Oregon, and we expect that most – if not all – Oregon-based fuel holding tanks and pipelines will be destroyed in a large earthquake," as this article warns.[60]

The reason is because of soil liquefaction, as noted previously. Regrettably, more than 90 percent of the state's fuel supply sits along a six-mile stretch in Northwest Portland's industrial district, as explained here.[61] The same article goes on to state that: "If that [soil liquefaction] happens here in Portland, it could devastate supply lines for fuel, electricity and natural gas. It could also mean a major chemical spill into the Willamette River" due, in part, to the fact that "many of the tanks are decades old and were built before seismic requirements in building codes."

There are supposed fixes to shore up soil where liquefaction is a distinct possibility—including underneath these crucial oil stores—such as by "injections of grout to make the soil less permeable, or installing stone columns within the ground," as further discussed here.[62] The problem with making this happen is twofold, in that, (1) nobody wants to foot the bill and (2) there's a regulatory gap, both of which indicate that nothing will change until the earthquake hits, all their fuel is lost, and we choose to rebuild with the next Cascadia event in mind.

Dams Deserve a Special Mention

The possibility for flooding and subsequent damage caused from dams breaking under the stress of a megaquake is something for all who live downstream to be keenly aware of. Realize that there are A LOT of dams in the Pacific Northwest. Apparently, Washington state has over 1100 dams, with King county alone (where Seattle is located) boasting over one hundred dams.[63] Oregon has several hundred dams as well.[64]

Of course, not all dams are created equal and most aren't even made from concrete. Some dams are quite small and should be expected to cause relatively little damage if ruptured whereas others, such as the Grand Coulee Dam west of Spokane, is one of the largest and will surely wreak havoc for dozens of miles downstream if it were to rupture.[65]

In fact, this *Living With Dams FEMA PDF* points out that dams could be serious trouble even without a major natural disaster affecting them: "If they are not maintained and operated correctly, dams can pose risks to those living downstream. When dams age, deteriorate, or malfunction, they can release sudden, dangerous flood flows. Dam failures can pose safety risks to an often unaware public. Many communities in the United States are in the vicinity of at least one dam. In many cases, large populations, vital elements of our infrastructure, jobs, and businesses are located downstream of dams. Dam failure floods are almost always more sudden and violent than normal stream, river, or coastal floods. They often produce damage that looks like tornado damage."[66]

Surprisingly, the same FEMA reference above points out that: "Foundation defects, including settlement and slope instability, or damage caused by earthquakes, have caused about 30 percent of all dam failures in the United States." I'd suspect we'll see an even higher rate of dam failures after minutes of sustained shaking and hundreds of aftershocks that follow a megaquake.

If interested, you can use this resource to learn more about high risk dams in Washington and Oregon (or any state, for that matter) and review this Dam Safety Performance Report for Washington state and the Dam Safety Performance Report for Oregon state.[67, 68, 69] What I find most concerning is that each state has hundreds of high hazard potential dams, meaning that their failure will result in loss of life and significant property damage!

And, although I couldn't find a good map for either state to link to, the above-referenced Dam Safety Performance Reports do have maps with colored dots on the first page that give some indication of where these potentially destructive dams are located. Suffice it to say, there are plenty of them all along and west of the I-5 corridor. We'll figure out how to find specific dams near you in part three.

Severely Delayed National Response

It used to be that FEMA advocated people be self-reliant for 72 hours because that was the anticipated response time from first responders and relief agencies, such as FEMA and the Red Cross, not to mention local responders. These days they tend to suggest two weeks of self-sufficiency, which is a more realistic expectation of response time for major disaster scenarios. Realize that a Cascadia event is NOT a "major" disaster scenario... it's a "nightmare" scenario.

Personally, I would encourage you to be prepared to survive on your own for as long as you can be, with weeks being the absolute minimum I could possibly suggest. In fact, with such a devastating scenario at hand, I would encourage those folks most likely to be affected by such an event to prepare to survive on their own for at least a month or two, if not longer.

I've perused Oregon state's resilience plan (who seem to be taking this a bit more seriously than my home state of Washington) and they're suggesting it will take months to restore most services for those living in the valley and, worse, three to six months to restore electrical services to the coast, one month to one year to restore drinking water and sewer services (I'd say that's optimistic), and up to three years to restore healthcare services. You and I both know how off government assessments can be... I would double those estimates just to be safe.[70]

Of course, this isn't to say that there will be NO power of any sort, anywhere along the Oregon coast for months, or that there will be NO healthcare facilities operating for years to come. These estimates are to get society relatively back to normal. Realistically we could expect some services to resume sporadically. Whether you'll be among those to benefit or not will remain to be seen. The same can be said for whether or not the services to resume are the services you need. That is, maybe they restored water first, but you needed power, or vice-versa. You get the idea.

Seeing as though the damage from a Cascadia event should dwarf any other natural disaster to ever hit the mainland United States, we really shouldn't look at relief agency response times to other major disasters, such as Hurricane Katrina or Hurricane Sandy, but that's the best we can do right now because we haven't seen anything worse in our lifetimes.

Due to a variety of factors, the Hurricane Katrina response may have been an anomaly. Clearly, the government failed to act quickly enough in many instances, often taking several days or longer to initially respond. Hurricane Sandy was a different story altogether, with FEMA and other agencies responding much faster, often within a day or two.

The thing is that relief agencies have days to prepare for hurricanes, to develop reaction plans, stage necessary supplies, coordinate with local agencies, and so on. That's just not possible with earthquakes. As such, don't expect "boots on the ground" hours or days after a Cascadia event. Remember, too, that many local emergency response agencies may need help themselves, which will certainly delay civilian aid substantially. Prepare yourself now.

1960 Chilean Case Study

Let's briefly look at the 1960 Valdivia, Chile earthquake because, as luck would have it, the earthquake and resulting tsunami in Chile is eerily similar in size and scope as to what could happen during a Cascadia event, as shown here.[71]

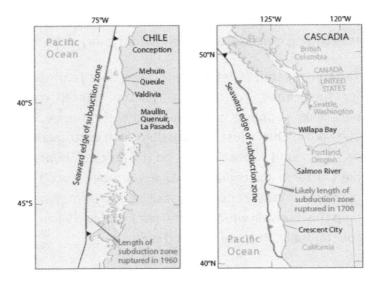

Figure 10

Interestingly, the U.S. Geological Survey (USGS) realized these similarities too and began collecting firsthand accounts of what happened from survivors; Here's a PDF summary of their findings, if interested.[72]

The Chilean megaquake was measured at between magnitude 9.4-9.6 and is the largest earthquake ever recorded; recall that a Cascadia event could easily be a magnitude 9.0 or greater. When using the USGS "How much bigger...?" calculator to compare them, we find that a magnitude 9.5 quake is about 3.1 times bigger than a magnitude 9.0, yet 5.6 times as strong in terms of energy release.[73] Regardless, a 9.0 megaquake is unlike anything we've experienced in modern history here on the U.S. mainland and should not be underestimated.

Anyway, the Chilean event killed thousands (estimates suggest up to several thousand), most of whom died after the initial megaquake, specifically from tsunami waves. Authorities anticipate a similar ratio of earthquake to tsunami death tolls here in America. As such, they recommend that you do anything and everything you can after an earthquake strikes to get to higher ground, and I do as well. They go so far as to suggest you literally climb a tree—good luck with that—or cling to debris if you have no other choice, and I would agree assuming you're completely desperate. This is where my agreement and the similarities end.

For starters, 1960's Chile is nothing like the modern-day Pacific Northwest. Sure, people in Chile had houses, stores, and some roads, but they didn't have anything like the infrastructure and modernization that we currently enjoy here in the United States. In a strange way, **Chile of nearly sixty years ago was better suited to survive such a megaquake because it was less modernized with far fewer people than we currently have here**. Even modern-day Chile has a population of only about eighteen million... we have about half that many people stuffed into the two major metropolitan areas of Seattle and Portland alone, as well as plenty more residents west of Interstate 5, all of whom are expected to be directly impacted.

Due, in large part, to our widespread use of—and reliance on—modern infrastructure, we will have a much more difficult time recovering than Chile did, and we will see much more damage as a result. Remember, authorities are already warning us that "everything west of I-5 will be toast" because:

- Aftershocks could further damage already weakened buildings and infrastructure, thereby making them a continuous hazard for weeks and months to come;
- Soil liquefaction and landslides will decimate major areas of crucial land, causing underground utilities to rise out of the ground when that happens too;
- Fuel holding tanks and pipelines will be destroyed, leaving Oregon with nothing to

rely upon, especially if Seattle-area refineries are severely damaged as well;

- Downed power lines and gas line ruptures will cause widespread fires (and smoke, which authorities seem to completely ignore);
- Floodwaters will bring massive amounts of debris and deadly diseases to the coast;
- Water, sewer, power, and other critical infrastructure will be severely damaged all along and west of Interstate 5, likely for months to come;
- Response times are anticipated to be seriously delayed because local first responders may not be able to respond or, worse, in need of help themselves.

Just imagine what they don't know because we've never experienced it. I can't say this enough: BE PREPARED TO SURVIVE ON YOUR OWN FOR A LONG TIME! If you get help long before then, that's great news. Just don't plan on help arriving days or even weeks after such an event because, if it doesn't, you're doing yourself a disservice when you could have prepared for it. Let's do that now…

PART 3

7 Survival Solutions to Keep You Safe

Hopefully by now you fully understand how dangerous a Cascadia event can be. I can't say for sure that the devastation will be as bad I warn, and I certainly hope it won't be. That said, we cannot assume the best-case scenario either. Rather, we must pray for the best and plan for the worst. Let's figure out how to plan for the worst now by dealing with the aforementioned problems in the order in which they were introduced, that being:

1. shaking from the initial earthquake;
2. the tsunami waves and flooding;
3. aftershocks;
4. damage from trees;
5. downed power lines and fires (e.g., from natural gas pipelines);
6. infrastructure problems and delayed response from first responders;
7. if you or family are away from home (this wasn't previously introduced).

Problem #1: Shaking from The Initial Earthquake

As we've discovered, the shaking from a Cascadia megathrust quake will likely be minutes in duration, far longer than traditional earthquakes most folks are accustomed to, and plenty of time to do considerable damage. That said, there are several actions we can take to help mitigate the potential damage, especially in our homes. We'll get to those in a moment but, first, let's talk about something you should be aware of...

My Problem With "Drop, Cover, and Hold On"

Perhaps you've heard about the controversy between the *drop, cover, and hold on* strategy versus the *triangle of life* strategy for earthquake survival. You haven't, you say? Great, because there isn't much of a controversy at all since the *drop, cover, and hold* on strategy is the recommended choice by authorities, but I'm getting ahead of myself. Let me briefly explain the two earthquake survival options here...

If you're unaware, the *drop, cover, and hold on* earthquake survival strategy is simply to drop to your hands and knees, cover your head and neck with one arm (though I'm not quite sure how you do that effectively), and hold on to something sturdy until the shaking stops. If possible, get under something sturdy or crawl next to an interior wall, away from windows.

The *triangle* of life alternative posits that, "building occupants should seek shelter near solid items that will provide a protective space, a void or space that could prevent injury or permit survival in the event of a major structural failure, a 'pancake collapse', and specifically advises against sheltering under tables."[74]

Ultimately, most experts agree that the *drop, cover, and hold on* strategy is far superior because, as this article points out, "The greatest danger is from falling and flying objects: Studies of injuries and deaths caused by earthquakes over the last several decades show that you are much more likely to be injured by falling or flying objects (TVs, lamps, glass, bookcases, etc.) than to die in a collapsed building. 'Drop, Cover, and Hold On' (as described above) will protect you from most of these injuries."[75]

During any normal earthquake I would certainly agree. Most injuries are going to be caused by items inside your home falling on your head rather than entire walls collapsing or the roof crashing down.

My problem with the *drop, cover, and hold on* strategy, however, is the expectation that there is something to take cover under. I wrote about this years ago but, for some reason, I called it the "duck, cover, and hold" method rather than the "drop, cover, and hold on" method as I should have, and I honestly have no idea what I was thinking about when I said "duck" instead of "drop."[76]

Regardless, the point is that, at least in my experience, there is very little furniture with which you can truly take cover underneath. At best you'll be taking cover next to a piece of furniture, which is more like the *triangle of life* strategy that the experts warn against.

I'm not advocating that the *triangle of life* method is a better option whatsoever; I am, on the other hand, merely suggesting that you may not have much choice in the matter. At the very least, your biggest concern is to cover your head as best as you can and to limit exposure of the rest of your body, if possible.

The question now is: what should you do during a Cascadia event?

My assumption is that, initially, this earthquake will start out like any other. As such, it will be items inside your home or workplace that move around or fall and are, therefore, most likely to injure you. (Note: there are many videos on YouTube that show how quickly your belongings can move around, especially large items, during an earthquake, if interested.) Clearly, the *drop, cover, and hold on* strategy is the right way to go here.

As the earthquake progresses, however, my "worst-case scenario" assumption is that the structure may begin to fail, as discussed earlier. Remember, we're preparing for the potential of walls to fall over and rooftops to collapse. If this happens then the *drop, cover, and hold on* strategy won't do you much good because, let's face it, your body is no match for thousands of pounds of wood falling on you. In this case, the *triangle of life* strategy may seem appropriate.

Honestly, though, when you're in the moment you're not going to be asking yourself which strategy you should take. With that in mind, you should begin to think about what you'll do and where the safest place in your home or workplace is should a major earthquake strike. Regardless of strategy employed, the safest place is almost always away from outside walls and windows, and closest to the ground. If that also means underneath or next to a sturdy table or even a couch, then so be it.

I'll finish by saying that, if you've ever been through an earthquake or if you've watched videos online, you'll notice that people can often move around during the initial moments of a quake. In fact, most people try to get outside (I've done so several times as a teenager) which is something that most experts say not to do.

As the earthquake progresses—and especially if you're closer to the epicenter—the shaking may be more intense, obstacles may be in your path, and it will be more difficult to move about as a result. You may, in fact, be unable to do anything but "drop, cover, and hold on." If this is the case, then do your best to take cover where you are, shielding your head until the shaking stops. If you expect to take shelter in a specific location, on the other hand, do so quickly because your ability to continue to move about will only get worse as the earthquake progresses. Again, the authorities recommend you do NOT move around! You've been warned.

Mitigating Earthquake Damage

By far the most important actions that you can take are those you take BEFORE an earthquake strikes. These are called mitigating actions. I have links on my website to a few useful files you can make use of— just scroll down to the "Earthquake Disaster Information" heading to see them—so I won't spend a lot of time on them here.[77]

Suffice it to say that, you're going to want to secure or even remove large items that can abruptly move or fall and easily hurt you or your family. This is why authorities tell you to do things like anchor large bookcases, dresser drawers, televisions, and the like. Items such as computers, pictures, and mirrors should be secured as well. Even drawers and cabinets could be latched so that whatever is inside doesn't come crashing out thereby making it very difficult to walk over or through, especially if their contents break or spill.

There's plenty more that can be done, including reinforcing foundations and chimneys, strapping down appliances (if not already required to do so by law), bracing cripple walls, and more. You really should consult a professional if you need to do any of these mitigating actions.

All the above is common knowledge for most people who know anything about earthquake safety. The trick is to take care of them now!

Staying Safe During the Quake

Besides the above actions, you should also think about how you will react to an earthquake in the moment. Considering each room in your home, where's the likeliest safest place to be? Is there a truly sturdy piece of furniture you can hide under? What about your family? Do they know what to do, especially young children? The same questions should be asked of your workplace, children's schools, or really any place you and your family frequent regularly.

We should also briefly consider the outside environment too. As I've mentioned, we happen to live amid many tall pine trees. Whereas it would have felt safest to be outside when we lived in California because there was nothing to come crashing down upon us, I would strongly reconsider going outside during an earthquake if you live among many trees, like I do. Remember, it's not just that entire trees may come crashing down, it's more likely that tree branches will snap, or tops of already unstable trees will give way.

Of course, you shouldn't be solely concerned with trees. Power lines could fall, yard equipment and even vehicles could severely injure you if you sought cover beside them... who knows. Go look around both inside and outside your home, then consider what may be a hazard to you and, if possible, do something about it.

Problem #2: The Tsunami Waves and Flooding

If you'll recall, scientists estimate that: "Seismic sea waves, or tsunamis, could be as high as thirty to forty feet with a magnitude 9 earthquake, but less than half that with an 8. Fifteen to thirty minutes after the mainshock had died away, the first of several tsunamis would strike... sweeping the sand from barrier bars inland, overwhelming beach houses and bayfront boutiques and restaurants as far as several blocks away from the sea. These destructive waves would be repeated several times," according to this article referenced earlier.[78]

I've even seen estimates that the first tsunami waves could strike within minutes depending on the location of the epicenter. Clearly, there won't be much time to move to higher ground regardless of what estimate you choose to accept. Fifteen minutes, in this case, isn't that long at all, especially when most people will be trying to wrap their heads' around what just happened, check on family and neighbors, and assess the damage to their home and belongings. You really need to have a plan to evacuate laid out in advance.

Remember, too, that it's not just those along the coastline who need to be concerned. And, while the flooding may take longer to reach other locations (such as the Puget Sound), if you live or work anywhere near the ocean, flood plains, or natural water ways along the coast, I would encourage you to get to higher ground as quickly as possible just to be safe.

If interested, this documentary about the flooding in Japan should help you understand just how devastating the flooding alone from a tsunami can be.[79] Being in and around floodwaters—even if they don't wash you away—is no place to be.

How to Stay Safe from Tsunami Flooding

There are two major actions you need to take now:

1. Plan a route to higher ground
2. Have supplies ready to take with you

Getting to higher ground may sound easy enough but, like I mentioned earlier, there could be plenty of obstacles in your way, from fallen trees and power lines to massive amounts of debris strewn from the earthquake damage, all of which will slow you down considerably. As such, it behooves you to have more than one route plotted to get to where you need to go. And, as I've discussed, expect to do so on foot since roadways could be impassable by vehicle.

If on foot, don't expect to cover much ground at all. Considering that the average walking speed (depending on a variety of factors) is about two or three miles per hour, you won't cover much ground at that pace. Worse, if we assume you're slowed down because of debris in your path or having to traverse difficult terrain, or if you have physical limitations, you may only be able to cover a half-mile or less per hour. That's not much distance when floodwaters can flow miles inland and do so at several miles per hour.

Thus, my advice would be to look for the nearest high ground, regardless of where it is that you want to get to. Estimates I've seen indicate that about one hundred feet in elevation should be high enough to avoid being directly affected by floodwaters, though, there's no harm in getting higher, if possible. Personally, I plan on getting at least two hundred feet above sea level, but we'd need to travel about three miles to get there. Fortunately, we can get above one hundred feet in a much shorter timeframe. We also happen to have more time to do so than those along the coastline; you'll want to plan how fast you need to move accordingly.

FYI, if you're not sure of your elevation, there are plenty of free elevation apps in the app store; I downloaded "My Elevation" by RDH Software, though, there are plenty of others. You could also use free online elevation maps too.[80]

The other major action you should take is to have some supplies ready to take with you in a backpack because you'll most likely be on foot. I won't go into detail here as I cover this topic extensively in my book, *53 Essential Bug Out Bag Supplies*, but you should have some extra clothing to keep you warm and dry, sneakers or decent shoes for walking, some snacks or food that doesn't need prepared, a water bottle (preferably filled), a few to several days of shelf-stable medications (as well as extra glasses or contacts), a flashlight with extra batteries, and maybe a bit of cash, to name the bare minimum that I can suggest.[81]

Remember supplies for young children and pets, if necessary, and ensure each able-bodied family member has their own bag to carry.

These supplies should be kept ready-to-go in a safe place inside your home. Granted, preparing for a major earthquake such as this may be a good reason to keep these bags away from your home, such as in your vehicle. I happen to do this because I like having these supplies in our vehicles for when we're away from home. Just be aware that any food or medications will go bad faster when not in a climate-controlled environment and, as such, will need replaced regularly, perhaps every few months.

I should also quickly mention the usefulness of caches. A cache is nothing more than some supplies—similar in nature to a bug out bag—which have been stored or stashed in a specific location, often hidden from view, that you can access after a disaster. These supplies could be stashed, for example, where you intend to evacuate to so that you have something to rely upon when you get there. Or, you could stash supplies along the intended evacuation route so that you have additional supplies to make use of. Just be aware that you cannot store caches on someone's property without permission and never on public land. FYI, small self-storage lockers make great, legal caches and can store a lot of supplies too, if this interests you.

Problem #3: Aftershocks

Recall that this article says we will see aftershocks which, "...are dangerous because they are usually unpredictable, can be of a large magnitude, and can collapse buildings that are damaged from the main shock. Bigger earthquakes have more and larger aftershocks and the sequences can last for years or even longer especially when a large event occurs in a seismically quiet area."[82]

The damage caused by aftershocks are nothing to ignore, largely because the aftershocks will continue to affect buildings and infrastructure which have already been heavily damaged by the initial megaquake. To put this in perspective, just imagine the magnitude 6.8 Loma Prieta earthquake (or worse) that I've mentioned earlier striking AFTER a magnitude 9.0 megaquake hits. How much additional damage would be done as a result? What if similar earthquakes strike repeatedly?

Sadly, there isn't much that you can do to prepare for these besides being keenly aware that they can and will happen, particularly in the hours and days after the mainshock: "An earthquake large enough to cause damage will probably produce several felt aftershocks within the first hour. The rate of aftershocks dies off quickly. The day after the mainshock has about half the aftershocks of the first day. Ten days after the mainshock there are only a tenth the number of aftershocks," according to this site.[83]

No doubt, you should be very cautious when entering potentially damaged structures or using them for shelter after the mainshock earthquake. Of course, we're not all certified structural engineers, so use an abundance of caution when entering buildings in the hours and days after... and wear a hard hat if you have one, I'm not kidding.

Problem #4: Damage from Trees

Many of us in the Pacific Northwest tend to love our trees. Regrettably, these same trees may cause an abundance of damage during a Cascadia event, from blocking roadways to damaging homes and even downing power lines... they will surely cause havoc for many. Remember, it's not just that entire trees may fall over; top-heavy trees could break in two, large tree branches will snap, and roadways may be covered with leaf litter making them nearly unrecognizable.

With regards to damage caused by trees to your home or other structures, there isn't much you can do here besides having large tarps to cover any major holes in rooftops, walls, etc. And, of course, to be very concerned about entering any structures which have been severely damaged in this manner.

To deal with blocked roadways by fallen trees or large branches—and assuming you can still get out by vehicle—you could employ a variety of devices, such as a vehicle winch, come-a-longs, and chainsaws. But, to be honest, if you're not already familiar with these tools then I wouldn't recommend them.

Instead, I would encourage you to have multiple evacuation routes as mentioned previously. This takes a lot of time to plan out and to get right. Essentially, you'll want to lay out a trusty local map (or use Google Maps) and begin to plot at least two or more distinct routes to a safer location, even if some of these routes take a circuitous path to get there. Remember, the sooner you can get to your evacuation spot the better because you're not only trying to avoid additional damage from seismic activity and flooding, but you're also trying to beat out other evacuees as well.

Now, considering that we're discussing the Pacific Northwest then you're going to want to, at minimum, get east of Interstate 5 and away from major cities such as Seattle, preferably, east of the Cascades where damage is anticipated to be less. If you're in northern California, then go south or east until it's clear the damage is minimal.

There's a lot more that can be covered with regards to such an evacuation (I cover a lot of that in my 12 Pillars of Survival course) but the general idea is to have several ways to get to a safe location, do so before everyone else does, and to have the supplies (e.g., food, money, gasoline) to see you through until you get there.[84]

Problem #5: Downed Power Lines and Fires

Downed power lines will be a massive problem for many after a Cascadia megaquake. After all, power lines could crash down on their own or be helped along by falling tree branches. Not only are they a danger to drive or walk over—here again is why you should never cross downed power lines—they will surely start some fires due to being in and among so many trees, and we already know that natural gas lines start one in four fires after an earthquake as well.[85] Recall, too, that first responders will be overwhelmed, undermanned, ill-equipped and, therefore, likely unable to put out most fires for days or weeks after. Who's to say how much of the landscape will have burned by then.

In my opinion, uncontrolled fires and the smoke produced from them could be an unexpected disaster in and of itself. To put this in perspective, the 1906 magnitude 7.9 earthquake that hit San Francisco had more damage from fires than the earthquake itself: "As damaging as the earthquake and its aftershocks were, the fires that burned out of control afterward were even more destructive. It has been estimated that up to 90% of the total destruction was the result of the subsequent fires. Within three days, over 30 fires, caused by ruptured gas mains, destroyed approximately 25,000 buildings on 490 city blocks...

In all, the fires burned for four days and nights," according to Wikipedia.[86]

Granted, there were other reasons that fires caused such damage in San Francisco, including foolishness by residents and even first responders. Expect your neighbors to start fires for a variety of reasons, from knocking over candles used for light to mishaps while cooking... it will be a mess.

To reduce the likelihood of your own property burning down, you can and should:

1. Install automatic shutoff valves and flexible connectors for gas and propane appliances.
2. Follow the wildfire advice given here (especially the PDF reference) to get your property ready or use this site to do so.[87, 88]

Smoke will be the other major problem. As property and woodlands continue to burn, smoke will fill the area and air quality will diminish, possibly making it difficult to breathe or even to see far off distances. This will be one more very good reason to have evacuated sooner rather than later. Surprisingly, those along the coastline may fare better than those inland because there will be less material to burn (because the Pacific Ocean is to the west) as well as a steady breeze blowing smoke further inland.

In this case, those who are relatively close to the Pacific coastline may find it better to evacuate west if they haven't been able to do so yet to avoid fires and smoke assuming, of course, that the floodwaters have receded or are not nearly as bad as anticipated. I can't say evacuating towards the coast will be the best course of action in all cases, but I can say it will be something to consider if you're unable to evacuate elsewhere initially.

If you do expect trouble breathing because of smoke inhalation, masks can help. For instance, N95 or N100 masks are popular options for evacuation packs—I keep several in our bags—but, to be honest, they're not very comfortable to wear for long periods of time, don't work well on children or those with facial hair, and don't filter out hazardous gasses (such as carbon monoxide, among others).

There are better options available, such as masks that have one-way exhalation valves and even expensive smoke hoods, but neither of these solutions work for long periods of time.[89, 90, 91] That is, you wouldn't expect to be able to wear them for weeks on end until the smoke dies down. About the best you can do if you're unable to evacuate is to stay indoors as much as possible.

Perhaps we'll get lucky and the Cascadia event will strike during the rainy season and most of the potential for fires will be minimal. Then again, it could hit during the summer months when we can go for weeks on end without a single drop of rain. I promise this will be the first and last time Pacific Northwest residents will pray for rain.

Problem #6: Infrastructure Problems and Delayed Response from First Responders

Infrastructure problems would mean concerns like not having water, food, power, garbage service, heat in the winter, medications, and so on. Delayed response from first responders would mean concerns like not having people around to deal with medical problems, cuts, burns, and so much more that could go wrong in the weeks and months following. You really must prepare to be on your own for weeks at minimum. This is known as "sheltering in place" or "hunkering down."

Remember, Oregon authorities suggest it will take months to restore most services to those directly affected, even years to restore truly functioning healthcare services.[92] Months may not sound that long, but when you have no expectation of replenishing your water or food supplies, may spend the entire winter without heat, and cannot get your necessary medications either... months may as well be decades.

Therefore, the first action you should take is to begin to stockpile all the necessary supplies you may need to survive for months in the event you're unable to evacuate. This would include:

- **Food** (particularly easy to make meals, such as canned food);
- **Water** (plus the ability to procure and properly treat more water);
- **Prescription medications** (especially life-necessary medications);
- **Fuel** (e.g., propane) or wood to cook or heat with.

There are plenty of other useful items you could include, such as batteries to run flashlights and radios, soap to keep from getting sick and to clean dishes or even clothes, and hygiene supplies to feel normal. This list of 100 items to disappear first often circulates the internet and may be a decent starting point but, truth be told, about half of the items on that list would be useless for most people because they simply wouldn't know what to do with them.[93]

Regarding the lack of first responders: besides knowing what to do by taking appropriate first aid courses and having appropriate first aid supplies, I would encourage you to get The Survival Medicine Handbook by Dr. Alton and his wife, Amy Alton.[94] It's about the best advice you'll find for dealing with medical problems post-disaster. And, of course, my survival course covers all the above problems and so much more too.[95]

Regarding Nearby Dams and Flooding

Though not every dam is listed—certain minimum requirements must be met to be included—you can use this reference to find out about nearby dam locations, if there are any... and the odds are that there will be.[96]

Unfortunately, using the above-referenced website isn't very intuitive, but eventually you'll want to get to the "Interactive Map" tab (which I cannot link to because the website won't allow it) and then zoom in over your location. You'll then want to expand the "Layers" section, choose "Corps of Engineers Data," and finally click "All NID Dams" to add that layer. Small blue squares should show up if there are any dams nearby in the database; if you don't see any you should try zooming out.

To find out more about individual dams, you should be able to click on them or just draw a larger square around the small blue squares with your mouse. Doing so should cause a popup to display with the dam name and other information, though nothing about its potential risk level is included; I've found that not every dam I tried to click on had additional information for whatever reason, so keep that in mind.

I should also mention that I used this website on my computer and NOT on a smartphone or tablet, so I don't know how well the data will be shown on them... and I'm not going to try because it was difficult enough to use with my computer.

Regardless, the idea with using this website is to help you decide if you have a nearby dam to be concerned with. You can, for example, discover a nearby dam name using the "Interactive Map" and then plug that data into the "NID Interactive Report" database on the same website to find out more.

From what I can gather, if you look for the "EAP" text (which stands for "Emergency Action Plan") if there's a "Y" next to it then that's a good indication that this dam is one to be concerned with for sure.

Granted, there could very well be other nearby dams not listed, so use this website as a good starting point in your research. If you do have a nearby dam that could be trouble, then you're going to want to treat this concern like the tsunami waves and flooding discussed in problem two previously. Remember, flooding from a ruptured dam could be every bit as devastating as flooding from tsunami waves, perhaps even more so because you're all but guaranteed to be affected if you live downstream of one!

Problem #7: You or Family Are Away from Home

Although I've alluded to this problem previously, I haven't specifically addressed it yet. That is, what should you do if you or family members are away from home when the disaster strikes, perhaps at work or school, or even in the car? Should everyone return home, attempt to evacuate on their own immediately, meet somewhere else first and then decide?

Well, as it turns out, the answer totally depends on your situation. For example, if you happen to live on the fringes of the expected disaster area, or it's clear that you weren't severely affected by the megaquake or tsunami flooding, then it may be best to return home, assess damage, gather supplies, help neighbors, and so on, then decide what to do from there.

If, however, you've been severely affected, it may be best for you to attempt to meet up first and to evacuate as quickly as possible afterwards rather than, for instance, to expect everyone to return home and then to evacuate together which could cost you precious time. In other cases, it may be best for everyone to evacuate on their own and meet at a designated "safe" spot east of the Cascades, for instance, days later.

No doubt this requires a lot of planning and consideration on your part. You really do need to sit down, talk with your family, and consider what you'll do. At the very least, **you should have an initial reaction plan and then a fallback plan**. That is, you may initially decide that everyone should return home and will decide what to do afterwards, but if the disaster is clearly more destructive than anticipated that everyone should be notified via text message, evacuate on their own initially, and finally meet at a specific location and time. There's easily more to consider than that since this is clearly an overgeneralization, but that's the idea briefly.

Other Considerations Not Yet Covered

Living on An Island

I recognize, too, that some of you reading this could live on an island as there are dozens of inhabited islands in the area. From what I can tell, many of these islands may be largely protected by larger land masses to the west, though, Vancouver Island could take a direct hit. For most other island inhabitants this is good news because it means that tsunami waves should be less likely to directly affect most folks who live on islands. Granted, this doesn't mean that you would be completely safe from flooding, just safe from the initial tsunami waves.

Therefore, you should move as far inland as possible or to the highest ground around if unable to do so. Alternatively, if you have a boat and you're able to access it rather quickly, you could be far better off sailing the waters for the next few days rather than on land because tsunami waves go largely unnoticed until they reach shallower waters near land. So long as you're clearly away from any shores you may not even realize the tsunami waves passed you by.

One other major problem with living on an island is that rescue efforts may take even longer to reach you because, like it or not, you would be less of a priority

9.0 Cascadia Earthquake Survival

since there will be more people to help on the mainland. As such, you should expect to be on your own for even longer than the rest of us.

What About Sailing Away?

Personally, I don't own a boat and I don't sail, so this isn't a plan that I have. That said, if you do have a relatively well-stocked boat—or if you can stock it with a week or two of provisions—and you're an experienced sailor, being on the water and sailing to a safe spot may be the best course of action, hands down.

After all, there will surely be far fewer people on the water than on land, you'd be able to travel much further on water than by foot or even by vehicle, and you'll clearly be insulated from the devastating aftermath, including aftershocks, fires, and a lack of resources, to name a few of the major concerns. I clearly need a boat, and maybe you do too.

The only major caution I would put forth is for those who live along the Pacific coast. Recall that tsunami waves may arrive to coastal areas mere minutes after the earthquake subsides depending on where the epicenter is located. As such, attempting to evacuate by boat may place you in greater danger unless, of course, you happen to already be aboard when the disaster strikes. Assuming you're not on a boat when the megaquake strikes, head inland if you're

100

anywhere along the coast, even if you have a boat to evacuate with.

Remember, too, that tsunami waves may strike repeatedly for hours after the initial onslaught, so, don't just assume that once the initial tsunami waves subside that it's safe to head to your boat. It may very well not be safe. For all others who may have more time to evacuate via boat, such as those living on islands nestled deep within in the Puget Sound, I would strongly consider evacuating via boat. That said, you should be quick about it and have an alternate evacuation plan as well.

Persons with Disabilities

If you have any sort of disability that limits your ability to function or to evacuate, you need to think even more strategically than the rest of us because, let's face it, you probably need more help from others or more time to get things done. For starters, this website offers some good advice for those with disabilities, mobility issues, and even senior citizens.[97]

Depending on the specific disability that you have, you'll have different problems to contend with. For those with mobility issues, for instance, your ability to evacuate quickly and safely will be paramount. As I've mentioned before, I anticipate that evacuation by vehicle will be almost impossible in many areas due to downed trees and power lines.

If this is the case for you then you need to think about what you're going to do. That is, will you still try to evacuate by vehicle and hope that the roads are passable? And, if they're not, will you take chances, such as crossing downed power lines? What if there are trees blocking the road? Are there other routes out of the area, even if it's not where you wanted to evacuate to initially? Do you have family or friends (or even neighbors) who can help you evacuate on foot? Do you trust them enough to come for you? What will you do if they don't?

Perhaps you're better off staying put. I know I said that one hundred feet is the anticipated safe elevation in most scenarios, but maybe I'm wrong and you'd be safe at fifty feet or even ten feet, especially if you don't live directly along the Pacific coastline. I can't say for sure; nobody can until it hits. But you do need to consider your course of action now.

The same can be said for any disability that may hinder your ability to cope with the aftermath of a disaster. If that means you need additional glasses or hearing aids (let's hope not, they're expensive) or even additional bottles of oxygen or very specific medications, now is the time to get that figured out while you have opportunity to do so.

Other Locations That Will Be Affected

While this book is mainly focused on Pacific Northwest residents, specifically those west of Interstate 5 in Washington, Oregon, and to a lesser extent, northern California, other locations and countries will be directly affected as well.

For starters, Vancouver Island in British Columbia may be as devastated as the rest of us. If you live here, you really need to prepare to be without support for long periods of time as well. The coastline along Alaska will see tsunami waves and Hawaii most certainly will too; even the southern half of California will see some activity as well.

In addition, many countries on the other side of the Pacific, namely Japan, will be affected by tsunami waves to one degree or another. This video simulation depicts how tsunami waves will propagate from the epicenter and travel throughout the Pacific Ocean.[98] Most of the initial damage will occur within roughly fifteen hours of the megaquake.

Fortunately, those further away from the epicenter—such as in Hawaii or Japan—should have ample warning to seek higher ground so long as they heed warning sirens and alerts.

Can the Cascadia Event Trigger the San Andreas or Yellowstone Eruption?

As it turns out, yes, it can trigger the San Andreas. According to this article: "…seismic activity on the southern Cascadia Subduction fault may have triggered major earthquakes along the northern San Andreas Fault," and that, "In a parallel study, they found that during the same period, 13 of these 15 San Andreas earthquakes occurred at almost the same time as earthquakes along the southern Cascadia Subduction Zone."[99]

The article goes on to state that: "'It's either an amazing coincidence or one fault triggered the other,' said Goldfinger. The generally larger size of the Cascadia earthquakes and the timing evidence suggests Cascadia may trigger the San Andreas.

So, there you have it… the Cascadia and San Andreas faults are apparently linked, at least, enough to suggest that one could trigger the other. The thing is that they may not be so linked that the rupture of one will instantly trigger the other hours later. Rather, it's a matter of decades (25 to 45 years, on average) and, therefore, California residents shouldn't immediately run for the hills when the Cascadia event hits.

What About Yellowstone?

When I'd first heard about this possibility, I'd thought to myself, "Oh no, that's a world-ending disaster! Could it be true?" This video, among others, attempt to answer that question.[100] What I like most about this video is the cross-section view that shows how the Juan de Fuca plate (as well as the smaller Gorda and Explorer plates which also contribute to the Cascadia megathrust zone) are attempting to subduct under the North American plate.

The video goes on to explain how some geologists believe that a fragment of a plate sits atop the Yellowstone magma chamber and acts as a lid or plug over the chamber. The idea is that a Cascadia quake could somehow trigger a Yellowstone eruption because they're interrelated via plate tectonics.

Interestingly, there is evidence that seismic events in the Pacific Northwest could directly affect Yellowstone. This article points out that: "In 2002 a 7.9 magnitude earthquake occurred in Central Alaska. The Denali fault, some 1,200 [miles] from Yellowstone ruptured sending shock waves south triggering hundreds of small earthquakes in The Yellowstone National Park."[101]

The evidence that a quake, even a megaquake, could trigger a full-blown Yellowstone eruption is speculation at best. I'd say that the best evidence we have is history itself. We know that Cascadia has erupted dozens of times in the past 10,000 years alone and that the last time Yellowstone erupted was about 640,000 years ago. If there is a connection between the two, it's not a strong one. As such, I wouldn't worry too much about Yellowstone erupting after a Cascadia event. And, if it did, that's a MUCH bigger problem than even a Cascadia megaquake.

Links to Helpful Websites

Although I referenced many good articles and websites throughout, I want to leave you with several more good resources to ensure you're as prepared as you can be for this.

For starters, you should know what your local emergency alert radio stations are.[102] A NOAA weather radio is a great idea too, just be sure you get a decent one that can be programmed to alert to specific hazards and to ignore others.[103]

Besides that, there are plenty of smartphone alert apps that you should have on your phone; I discuss all of them inside my book, *27 Crucial Smartphone Apps for Survival*, if you'd like to know which ones to get.[104] At the very least, you want apps that can alert you to disaster threats. The "NOAA Weather" app by Pandamonium Software is a good one to start with and one that I use, though, there are others to consider as well.

Also, here's a few good websites to make further use of:

- Shake Out (earthquake safety)[105]
- Earthquake Country Alliance (earthquake safety)[106]
- Oregon Seismic Predictions by Zip Code (doesn't work outside of Oregon state)[107]
- Pacific Tsunami Warning Center (referenced earlier, but good overall tsunami info)[108]

Final Thoughts

Let me be honest: before I began to research this topic myself, I'd had visions of major metropolitan areas being swallowed whole, several-hundred-foot waves crashing down on coastal cities, and Biblical-style flooding as far as the eye could see. Well, maybe it wasn't going to be quite THAT bad, I'd told myself, but I definitely let my imagination run wild for too long. The movies sure don't help paint a realistic picture of natural disasters, that's for sure.

It's enough to make one consider moving far away from here, and I've surely contemplated doing so. But that's an unrealistic reaction to an uncertain future for most of us, me included. Whereas it's one thing to move from one home to another while still living in the same geographic area, it's quite another to completely uproot one's family and move entirely out of the affected area when there's no guarantee such an event will happen in our lifetimes. After all, we have our roots here, jobs, schools, family, and friends... and I'm sure you do as well.

Now let me be clear: after researching the Cascadia event I've come to realize that, although there will be widespread destruction unlike anything we've seen here in America to be sure, this is likely a survivable event for most of us and that's a good starting point.

And, while the Cascadia event won't be anything like the movies, it won't be a walk in the park either.

So long as you've acted as outlined above (e.g., mitigated earthquake damage around your home, planned bug out routes) and you've secure the supplies to see you through, there's no reason why you and your family shouldn't be ready for the worst disaster ever.

Remember that you MUST ACT NOW because waiting until the megaquake strikes is literally too late! It won't take long to get yourself ready, and you'll likely be far better prepared to survive other natural disasters too. It's a win-win in anyone's book. I've shown you what you can do from my perspective, it's up to you to make the rest happen. If you'd like my thoughts consolidated into a single reference, grab your checklist below...

Get Your Free Checklist Here

Before you grab your checklist, be a good friend or family member and choose to help others who could use this crucial information...

Spread the Word, Share the Knowledge

I'm willing to bet that you have family and friends who could benefit from this book as well, so please take a moment right now and quickly share a link to it on Facebook, Twitter, or Pinterest... you can easily do so here.[109]

Now, download your free, easy-to-reference earthquake safety checklist here.[110]

Discover More Survival Books Here

If you liked what you read within then you're going to love my other survival books.[111] Here's a sampling:

- 53 Essential Bug Out Bag Supplies[112]
- 47 Easy DIY Survival Projects[113]
- The Complete Pet Safety Action Plan[114]
- 28 Powerful Home Security Solutions[115]
- 27 Crucial Smartphone Apps for Survival[116]
- 57 Scientifically-Proven Survival Foods to Stockpile[117]
- 75 of the Best Secret Hiding Places[118]
- Your Identity Theft Protection Game Plan[119]
- 144 Survival Uses for 10 Common Items[120]

And if you would like to be among the first to know when new survival books become available, fill out this form and you'll be notified via email.[121]

Recommended for You...

I want to point out one book from the above list, in particular, since you now clearly recognize the importance of evacuation during a Cascadia event: *53 Essential Bug Out Bag Supplies: How to Build a Suburban "Go Bag" You Can Rely Upon.*

Sadly, most every bug out bag list has some unwritten expectation that you'll be evacuating into a plentiful nearby wilderness with fish to catch, streams to rest alongside, mountains to navigate, and debris huts to build.

This just isn't the case for most of us.

Most Americans are going to be slogging their way through the urban "jungle" with nothing to catch for food or even a good source of water to drink! There may even be potentially unrecognizable building and roads as well as a shortage of safe shelter spots to get out of the elements.

These juxtapositions in bug out environments are quite different and should be treated as such. Discover precisely how to create a "go bag" you can rely upon in a suburban environment.[122]

Your Opinion Matters to Me

I'd love to hear your feedback about this book, especially anything I might be able to add or improve upon for future revisions. Please send me an email at rethinksurvival@gmail.com with the word "book" in the subject if you have something for me. (And be sure to include the book title so I'm not confused.)

Why You Should Review This Book...

Because reviews are critical in spreading the word about books, I ask that you take a moment and write a review of the book so that others know what to expect, particularly if you've found my advice useful.[123]

I do hope that you've enjoyed this book and that you will choose to implement my recommendations to help you and your family stay safe from the biggest disaster ever to hit the mainland United States.

I encourage you to please take a moment and download the checklist above, share this book with your friends and family using the link I provided previously, and leave a quick review on Amazon.com while you're at it.

May God bless you and your family. Thank you for your time, Damian.

List of Figures

Figure 1

Title, Description: USGS photo from 1989 Loma Prieta earthquake.
Author: H.G. Wilshire, U.S. Geological Survey.
Image Source:
https://commons.wikimedia.org/wiki/File:Cypress_structure.jpeg[124]
License: Public Domain.
Modifications: Image cropped.

Figure 2

Title, Description: FileMap of earthquakes in 2017.
Author: Phoenix7777.
Image Source:
https://commons.wikimedia.org/wiki/File:Map_of_earthquakes_in_2017.svg[125]
License: Creative Commons Attribution-Share Alike 4.0 International license.
Modifications: No changes were made to this image.

Figure 3

Title, Description: United States earthquake map.
Author: Wikideas1.
Image Source:
https://commons.wikimedia.org/wiki/File:Earthquake_map.jpeg[126]

Figure 4

Title, Description: A map of the Juan de Fuca plate.
Author: Alataristarion.
Image Source:
https://commons.wikimedia.org/wiki/File:JuanDeFu
caPlate.png[127]
License: Creative Commons Attribution-Share Alike
4.0 International license.
Modifications: Image cropped.

Figure 5

Title, Description: Earthquake potential off the West
coast of Washington and British Columbia.
Author: Webber assumed (based on copyright
claims).
Image Source:
https://commons.wikimedia.org/wiki/File:Juan_de_F
uca_Plate.jpg[128]
License: Public Domain.
Modifications: No changes were made to this image.

Figure 6

Title, Description: Cascadia subduction zone.
Author: The original uploader was Curps at English
Wikipedia.
Image Source:

https://commons.wikimedia.org/wiki/File:Cascadia_subduction_zone_USGS.png[129]
License: Public Domain.
Modifications: No changes were made to this image.

Figure 7

Title, Description: Collapsed Cypress Street Viaduct in Oakland, from the 1989 Loma Prieta earthquake.
Author: H.G. Wilshire, U.S. Geological Survey.
Image Source:
https://commons.wikimedia.org/wiki/File:022srUSGSCyprusVia.jpg[130]
License: Public Domain.
Modifications: No changes were made to this image.

Figure 8

Title, Description: Airmen from the 33rd Rescue Squadron spot a boat tossed on its side amidst residential buildings and other debris in northeastern Japan, March 14. The HH-60G Pave Hawk helicopter crew surveyed the damaged area as part of Japan's earthquake and tsunami recovery effort.
Author: U.S. Air Force photo/ Airman 1st Class Katrina R. Menchaca.
Image Source:
http://www.kadena.af.mil/News/Photos/igphoto/2000277172/mediaid/514347/[131]

License: Unknown.
Modifications: Image cropped.

Figure 9

Title, Description: Photo of power lines at
intersection.
Author: Damian Brindle.
Image Source: My photo.
License: None.
Modifications: No changes were made to this image.

Figure 10

Title, Description: Both the 1960 Chile earthquake
and the 1700 Cascadia earthquake were caused by
sudden ruptures of long segments of subduction
zones. Each of these quakes generated a tsunami
that not only struck nearby coastal areas but also
caused damage in coastal areas as far away as Japan.
Author: U.S. Geological Survey.
Image Source: https://pubs.usgs.gov/circ/c1187/[132]

License: Public Domain.
Modifications: No changes were made to this image.

Appendices

Appendix A: 30-Point Checklist

Appendix B: List of Resources

Appendix A: 30-Point Checklist

Problem #1: Shaking from the Initial Earthquake

1. Remember that "drop, cover, and hold on" is usually the best strategy: drop to your hands and knees, cover head and neck with one arm, and hold on to something sturdy.
2. Get under something sturdy or crawl next to an interior wall, away from windows, if possible.
3. Decide where the safest place in your home and workplace is; do this for each room as well, should you be unable to get to the safest place.
4. Secure all large items (e.g., bookcases, dresser drawers, televisions, desktop computers, etc.) as well as smaller items, including pictures and mirrors, because these are the most likely injuries.
5. Consider additional latches for drawers and cabinets to keep their contents contains so that they don't hurt you or make it difficult to walk over if the contents break or spill.
6. Ensure your home meets local building code requirements for earthquake safety and that major appliances, such as water heaters, are strapped down.
7. Be wary about going outside during an earthquake as there are many potential hazards

there too, including falling tree branches, yard equipment, vehicles, etc.

Problem #2: The Tsunami Waves and Flooding

1. Plan multiple routes to higher ground if you live anywhere near the coastline or waterways connected to it; I suggest a minimum of 100 feet above sea level.
2. Be prepared to walk out, as roadways may be impassable due to downed power lines and trees.
3. Gather necessary supplies—e.g., clothes, food, water, medications, etc.—and keep them in a bug out bag so you're ready to go at a moment's notice.
4. Consider caching supplies near your evacuation location (and even along your intended routes) so you have more to rely upon later.

Problem #3: Aftershocks

1. Be aware that aftershocks can be nearly as bad as the mainshock, and that we could have several within the first hour afterwards; some aftershocks could further damage structures that seemed to survive the initial earthquake making them unsafe to enter or be near.
2. Be extremely cautious when entering any potentially damaged structure or taking shelter inside until it can be properly assessed by a structural engineer; at least wear a hard hat.

Problem #4: Damage from Trees

1. Have a few tarps (and appropriate cordage, etc.) to cover holes in rooftops or walls caused by damage from fallen tree branches or entire trees.
2. Consider devices to remove downed trees, such as a vehicle winch, come-a-longs, and chainsaws, but only if you have experience using them.
3. Have multiple evacuation routes so you have the possibility of avoiding blocked roadways.
4. Attempt to evacuate east as fast as you can, preferably east of the Cascades, but even east of Interstate 5 is likely better than being west of it.

Problem #5: Downed Power Lines and Fires

1. Recall why you should never cross downed power lines.[133]
2. Install automatic shutoff valves and flexible connectors for gas and propane appliances.
3. Know how to turn off your own gas lines and have the tool to so safely.[134]
4. Follow the wildfire advice given here (especially the PDF reference) to get your property ready or use this site to do so.[135, 136]
5. Be able to minimize smoke inhalation with particulate masks or smoke hoods, if necessary.
6. Evacuate ASAP to avoid smoke and fire concerns, even consider going west to the Pacific Ocean if you can't get to the east of the Cascades.

Problem #6: Infrastructure Problems and Delayed Response from First Responders

1. Stockpile weeks or, preferably, months of necessary supplies, including food, water, prescription medications, and fuel (for cooking and warmth), to name the most important items.
2. Gather other useful items, such as batteries, soap, and hygiene supplies.
3. Have some knowledge of how to perform basic first aid, gather necessary supplies, and consider The Survival Medicine Handbook as a great resource for post-disaster medical knowledge.[137]

Problem #7: You or Family Are Away from Home + Other Considerations

1. Decide on your initial reaction plan as well as your fallback plan for responding to this event.
2. If you live on an island, get as far inland (and to higher ground) as you can because you may be inundated with floodwaters which bring both unwanted debris and deadly diseases.
3. If you have a boat, consider riding out the tsunami waves—and certainly to evacuate—by sea.
4. If you have any sort of disability, especially mobility concerns, decide now how you will respond to this event because roadways may be impassable.

Appendix B: List of Resources

- Link 1: https://rethinksurvival.com/books/earthquake-checklist.php
- Link 2: https://rethinksurvival.com/books/earthquake-book-offer.php
- Link 3: https://rethinksurvival.com/kindle-books/
- Link 4: https://www.nbcbayarea.com/news/local/Will-California-Fall-Into-the-Ocean-119434794.html
- Link 5: https://en.wikipedia.org/wiki/1906_San_Francisco_earthquake
- Link 6: https://en.wikipedia.org/wiki/1989_Loma_Prieta_earthquake
- Link 7: https://en.wikipedia.org/wiki/Lists_of_earthquakes#Deadliest_earthquakes
- Link 8: https://en.wikipedia.org/wiki/List_of_earthquakes_in_the_United_States
- Link 9: https://www.youtube.com/watch?v=e7ho6z32yyo

- Link 10:
  https://www.youtube.com/watch?v=FIgksa3
  x11w
- Link 11:
  https://en.wikipedia.org/wiki/Richter_magni
  tude_scale
- Link 12:
  https://en.wikipedia.org/wiki/Moment_mag
  nitude_scale
- Link 13:
  https://earthquake.usgs.gov/learn/topics/calc
  ulator.php
- Link 14:
  https://en.wikipedia.org/wiki/Lists_of_earth
  quakes#Largest_earthquakes_by_magnitude
- Link 15:
  http://www.sciencemag.org/news/2016/09/s
  cientists-may-have-solved-mystery-giant-
  midwest-earthquakes
- Link 16:
  https://en.wikipedia.org/wiki/List_of_earthq
  uakes_in_the_United_States
- Link 17:
  https://www.seattletimes.com/seattle-
  news/how-often-does-cascadia-fault-rip-
  scientists-disagree/
- Link 18:
  https://www.statesmanjournal.com/story/ne
  ws/2016/04/17/side--side-comparison-
  dueling-faults/83087478/

- Link 19:
  https://en.wikipedia.org/wiki/Megathrust_ea
  rthquake
- Link 20:
  http://www.newsweek.com/pacific-
  northwest-may-be-most-risk-big-one-due-
  seafloor-sediments-717632
- Link 21:
  https://patch.com/washington/seattle/risk-
  cascadia-quake-elevated-puget-sound-slow-
  slip-event-begins
- Link 22:
  https://tremor.pnsn.org/REALTIME/
- Link 23:
  https://hazards.uw.edu/geology/m9/
- Link 24: http://www.newsweek.com/really-
  big-earthquake-coming-striking-7-million-
  people-worst-natural-disaster-693318
- Link 25:
  http://www.washington.edu/news/2017/10/2
  3/50-simulations-of-the-really-big-one-
  show-how-a-9-0-cascadia-earthquake-
  could-play-out/
- Link 26:
  http://nwnewsnetwork.org/post/portland-
  earthquake-study-estimates-wide-variation-
  impact-depending-timing
- Link 27: https://www.shakealert.org/
- Link 28:
  https://www.seattletimes.com/seattle-

news/science/earthquake-early-warning-system-comes-to-washington-but-its-not-for-the-public-yet/
- Link 29:
https://www.seattletimes.com/seattle-news/warning-system-worked-but-is-it-worth-the-cost/
- Link 30:
http://www.newsweek.com/earthquake-prediction-based-rumbling-rocks-could-warn-disaster-week-advance-691657
- Link 31:
https://www.newyorker.com/magazine/2015/07/20/the-really-big-one
- Link 32:
http://www.washington.edu/news/2017/10/23/50-simulations-of-the-really-big-one-show-how-a-9-0-cascadia-earthquake-could-play-out/
- Link 33:
https://en.wikipedia.org/wiki/Soil_liquefaction
- Link 34:
https://www.seattletimes.com/seattle-news/times-watchdog/7-things-you-need-to-know-about-buildings-that-could-kill-in-a-major-earthquake/
- Link 35:
https://www.npr.org/templates/story/story.php?storyId=156841685

- Link 36:
  https://www.pbs.org/newshour/show/would-a-major-earthquake-sink-portland-in-liquefied-soil#transcript
- Link 37:
  https://www.youtube.com/watch?v=zhR6iuksuZw&t=1m02s
- Link 38:
  https://www.youtube.com/watch?v=tF204Pgf-eo
- Link 39:
  https://www.youtube.com/watch?v=W2WNFfem0TM
- Link 40:
  https://simplesupports.com/2017/08/24/us-vs-japanese-building-codes/
- Link 41:
  https://www.youtube.com/watch?v=7Zw-BvKo0pI
- Link 42:
  https://en.wikipedia.org/wiki/1700_Cascadia_earthquake
- Link 43:
  https://www.youtube.com/watch?v=spg62-MrYpQ
- Link 44:
  https://www.youtube.com/watch?v=5K6evRtpdAw

- Link 45:
  https://www.livescience.com/39110-japan-2011-earthquake-tsunami-facts.html
- Link 46:
  http://oregonstate.edu/instruct/oer/earthquake/05 chapter 4_color.html
- Link 47: http://ptwc.weather.gov/faq.php
- Link 48:
  https://www.livescience.com/37497-no-outrunning-tsunami.html
- Link 49:
  https://www.geekwire.com/2015/earthquake-experts-on-the-really-big-one-heres-what-will-actually-happen-in-seattle/
- Link 50:
  https://en.wikipedia.org/wiki/Aftershock
- Link 51:
  https://en.wikipedia.org/wiki/Foreshock
- Link 52:
  https://pnsn.org/outreach/faq/earthquake-prediction
- Link 53:
  https://www.youtube.com/watch?v=J99Vjk KaunA
- Link 54:
  https://www.pge.com/en_US/safety/electrical-safety/what-to-do-if-you-see-a-downed-power-line/what-to-do-if-you-see-a-downed-power-line.page

- Link 55: https://www.earthquakecountry.org/step1/gassafety/
- Link 56: https://rethinksurvival.com/kindle-books/earthquake-recommends/#wrench
- Link 57: http://nwnewsnetwork.org/post/portland-earthquake-study-estimates-wide-variation-impact-depending-timing
- Link 58: https://mil.wa.gov/uploads/pdf/HAZ-MIT-PLAN/Hazardous_Materials_Hazard_Profile.pdf
- Link 59: https://www.nbcnews.com/news/us-news/welcome-most-toxic-place-america-n689141
- Link 60: https://energyinfo.oregon.gov/2016/06/14/cascadia-rising/
- Link 61: https://www.opb.org/news/series/unprepared/oregon-earthquake-fuel-breakdown-90-percent/
- Link 62: https://www.opb.org/news/series/unprepared/oregon-earthquake-fuel-breakdown-90-percent/

- Link 63:
  https://en.wikipedia.org/wiki/List_of_dams_
  and_reservoirs_in_Washington
- Link 64:
  https://databasin.org/maps/f7f5ee6826ba4d7
  2a71690f660987a48
- Link 65:
  https://www.nps.gov/articles/washington-
  grand-coulee-dam.htm
- Link 66: https://www.fema.gov/media-
  library-data/20130726-1845-25045-
  7939/fema_p_956_living_with_dams.pdf
- Link 67: https://damsafety.org/states
- Link 68:
  https://damsafety.org/sites/default/files/WA
  _PerfomanceReport_v2.pdf
- Link 69:
  https://damsafety.org/sites/default/files/OR_
  PerfomanceReport_v2.pdf
- Link 70:
  http://www.geologictrips.com/rv/rvgtce.htm
- Link 71:
  https://en.wikipedia.org/wiki/1960_Valdivia
  _earthquake
- Link 72:
  http://www.disastersrus.org/emtools/tsunam
  i/USGSCircular_1187_rev2005_small.pdf
- Link 73:
  https://earthquake.usgs.gov/learn/topics/calc
  ulator.php

- Link 74: https://en.wikipedia.org/wiki/Triangle_of_Life
- Link 75: http://www.earthquakecountry.org/dropcoverholdon/
- Link 76: https://rethinksurvival.com/duck-cover-hold-earthquakes/
- Link 77: https://rethinksurvival.com/disaster-information/
- Link 78: http://oregonstate.edu/instruct/oer/earthquake/05 chapter 4_color.html
- Link 79: https://www.youtube.com/watch?v=Ti7nZwxUEjU
- Link 80: https://www.freemaptools.com/elevation-finder.htm
- Link 81: https://rethinksurvival.com/kindle-books/bug-out-bag-book/
- Link 82: https://en.wikipedia.org/wiki/Aftershock
- Link 83: http://scecinfo.usc.edu/eqcountry/roots/basics.html
- Link 84: https://rethinksurvival.com/books/get-12-pillars-of-survival.php

- Link 85: https://www.pge.com/en_US/safety/electrical-safety/what-to-do-if-you-see-a-downed-power-line/what-to-do-if-you-see-a-downed-power-line.page
- Link 86: https://en.wikipedia.org/wiki/1906_San_Francisco_earthquake#Fires
- Link 87: https://rethinksurvival.com/disaster-information/
- Link 88: http://www.readyforwildfire.org/
- Link 89: https://www.cdc.gov/niosh/npptl/topics/respirators/factsheets/respfact.html
- Link 90: https://rethinksurvival.com/kindle-books/earthquake-recommends/#mask
- Link 91: https://rethinksurvival.com/kindle-books/earthquake-recommends/#hood
- Link 92: http://www.geologictrips.com/rv/rvgtce.htm
- Link 93: http://www.thepowerhour.com/news/items_disappearfirst.htm
- Link 94: https://rethinksurvival.com/kindle-books/earthquake-recommends/#book
- Link 95: https://rethinksurvival.com/books/get-12-pillars-of-survival.php
- Link 96: http://nid.usace.army.mil/

- Link 97: https://www.earthquakecountry.org/disability/
- Link 98: https://www.youtube.com/watch?v=4W2iU10VB8c
- Link 99: https://www.offshore-mag.com/articles/print/volume-76/issue-1/geology-geophysics/research-shows-link-between-san-andreas-and-cascadia-faults.html
- Link 100: https://www.youtube.com/watch?v=FRoBVd-AO0k
- Link 101: http://undergroundmedic.com/2016/04/if-a-7-9-earthquake-in-alaska-can-affect-yellowstone-what-could-the-cascadia-or-san-andreas-do-to-it/
- Link 102: http://www.theradiosource.com/resources/stations-alert.htm
- Link 103: https://rethinksurvival.com/kindle-books/earthquake-recommends/#radio
- Link 104: https://rethinksurvival.com/kindle-books/smartphone-survival-apps-book/
- Link 105: https://www.shakeout.org/

- Link 106: http://www.earthquakecountry.org/
- Link 107: https://www.opb.org/news/widget/aftershoc k-find-your-cascadia-earthquake-story/
- Link 108: http://ptwc.weather.gov/
- Link 109: https://rethinksurvival.com/books/earthquak e-share.html
- Link 110: https://rethinksurvival.com/books/earthquak e-checklist.php
- Link 111: https://rethinksurvival.com/kindle-books/
- Link 112: https://rethinksurvival.com/kindle-books/bug-out-bag-book/
- Link 113: https://rethinksurvival.com/kindle-books/diy-survival-projects-book/
- Link 114: https://rethinksurvival.com/kindle-books/pet-safety-plan-book/
- Link 115: https://rethinksurvival.com/kindle-books/home-security-book/
- Link 116: https://rethinksurvival.com/kindle-books/smartphone-survival-apps-book/

- Link 117: https://rethinksurvival.com/kindle-books/survival-foods-book/
- Link 118: https://rethinksurvival.com/kindle-books/secret-hides-book/
- Link 119: https://rethinksurvival.com/kindle-books/id-theft-book/
- Link 120: https://rethinksurvival.com/kindle-books/survival-uses-book/
- Link 121: https://rethinksurvival.com/books/new-survival-books.php
- Link 122: https://rethinksurvival.com/kindle-books/bug-out-bag-book/
- Link 123: https://rethinksurvival.com/books/earthquake-review.php
- Link 124: https://commons.wikimedia.org/wiki/File:Cypress_structure.jpeg
- Link 125: https://commons.wikimedia.org/wiki/File:Map_of_earthquakes_in_2017.svg
- Link 126: https://commons.wikimedia.org/wiki/File:Earthquake_map.jpeg

- Link 127: https://commons.wikimedia.org/wiki/File:JuanDeFucaPlate.png
- Link 128: https://commons.wikimedia.org/wiki/File:Juan_de_Fuca_Plate.jpg
- Link 129: https://commons.wikimedia.org/wiki/File:Cascadia_subduction_zone_USGS.png
- Link 130: https://commons.wikimedia.org/wiki/File:022srUSGSCyprusVia.jpg
- Link 131: http://www.kadena.af.mil/News/Photos/igphoto/2000277172/mediaid/514347/
- Link 132: https://pubs.usgs.gov/circ/c1187/
- Link 133: https://www.pge.com/en_US/safety/electrical-safety/what-to-do-if-you-see-a-downed-power-line/what-to-do-if-you-see-a-downed-power-line.page
- Link 134: https://rethinksurvival.com/kindle-books/earthquake-recommends/#wrench
- Link 135: https://rethinksurvival.com/disaster-information/
- Link 136: http://www.readyforwildfire.org/

- Link 137: https://rethinksurvival.com/kindle-books/earthquake-recommends/#book

Made in the USA
Monee, IL
15 June 2020